Secrets of a Medium

Secrets of a Medium

Larry Dreller

WEISERBOOKS

Boston, MA/York Beach, ME

First published in 2003 by
Red Wheel/Weiser, LLC
York Beach, ME
With offices at:
368 Congress Street
Boston, MA 02210
www.redwheelweiser.com

Library of Congress Cataloging-in-Publication Data

Dreller, Larry.
  Secrets of a medium / Larry Dreller.
    p. cm.
  Includes bibliographical references.
  ISBN 1-57863-283-8
  1. Parapsychology. 2. Mediums. 3. Spiritual life. I. Title.
  BF1031.D69 2003
  133.9'1--dc21

                              2003008669

Typeset in Minion

PRINTED IN CANADA

TCP

10 09 08 07 06 05 04 03
 8 7 6 5 4 3 2 1

❦

This book is dedicated to Princess Diana,
whose light continues to brighten the heavens,
and to the torch bearers and modern-day saints who work
in hospices throughout the world, not for earthly fame and fortune,
but instead, sharing their love and caring—
and the sweat of compassion from their brow.

Millions of spiritual Creatures walk this Earth Unseen,
both when we wake, and when we sleep.
—JOHN MILTON, *Paradise Lost*

Contents

Introduction

It is an empirical fact that we must eventually depart this life—willingly, suddenly, or in struggle. Few of us, unless we are in terrible physical or emotional pain, feel that death holds the release and promise of excitement and adventure. Death for human beings will not be joyfully approached as the next great passage. Such an idea is against our basic nature and imprinted survival instinct. Life is; death is. There simply is no escape from our mortality—or so many people reason.

Then there are those poetic souls among us who compare our life to the rose. The bud springs forth, slowly opening while perfuming the air with its magnificence, and while it transitions through its short cycle of being, slowly or rapidly, it discards fragrant petals one by one, then dies. The rose has shared its beauty and fragrance with the world—that is, with those who take the time to witness its fusillade of glory. and although the rose continues to live on in mental imagery, through its brief visit in our personal universe, we realize the order of nature: we are born, we strive to live, then we are extinguished. Notice, however, that the fallen petals continue to emit a delicate fragrance while still flaunting their faded beauty—even when dried.

Spiritual human beings sense that our life cycle is more complicated, meaningful, and mission-driven than the flora and fauna of our planet. Our compressed existence demands relevance and purpose, and some of us are well assured that we shall again "live" after death, just in another form and in a different place. Those of us with belief, faith, and expectancy for an afterlife do not fear oblivion. Cold-hearted logic and skepticism is for the faithless, we believe: "Grave, where is thy victory?"

This book was not written as a mind-boggling revelation—so many authors are much better at this than I am. This volume primarily was written for those individuals who've come to the conclusion that human beings are not a mere coincidence or accident of the universe. We believe we were created for a purpose and that this purpose continues into a new world—an afterlife achieved by living a life based on spirituality and belief. We believe that human beings are much more than stew meat in the great cosmic soup bowl. Nor do we accept the fatalistic premise that death is a transcendental journey filled with existential despair and remorse. Science, technology, and worldwide theologies do not divide us in conjecture, or even unite us. We're begrudged the morsels and the few handfuls of crumbs we receive from their tables. They fail to answer the key questions we hunger for: What is my purpose? Where am I going after I die? We know that we must not denigrate our life experience to that of a successful or unsuccessful garden party.

How do we create and live our reality in a world filled with illusion? Science and techno-materialism appears logical and comfortable to a point—that is, if there are no in-depth questions about death and transfiguration, that final journey into eternity. The bottom line is this: There has to be some sort of continuity.

The theme of this book is to disregard the so-called reality that has been served to us, thereby forcing us into searching different directions for answers. This author will not attempt to rephrase the concepts of the shape, size, and origin of the universe or debate matter, time, or theologies, but will hopefully unleash the possibilities that await all of us on our demise, while bending minds and thoughts in the process. Metaphysical and paranormal explanations are similar to an attempt at containing water in open hands—however, it can be done! As intelligent children of the universe, we know that everything, regardless of its vastness, holds seeds of divergent possibilities and alternate explanations. Therefore, it is always up to us to make the changes in the adjustments of our realities.

This book is not intended to be a compendium of rituals; instead, it offers thoughts on how to draw things together. For those researching basic ideas on the paranormal, especially on mediumship, a basic guide does exist: *Beginner's Guide to Mediumship,* by this author and same publisher.

This book focuses on spirituality with purposeful intent, because spirituality is the key ingredient to a successful and meaningful life and the subsequent passage to the otherside. Karma, or whatever you want to call it, is also a very important cornerstone of life, that is, the principle of "The Golden Rule" and that what you sow, you will surely reap. These caveats are for everyone, not just the medium, but it is a hopeful expectation that mediums will incorporate these thoughts and principles into every reading.

We are all hungry souls seeking the great truths and solving the grand mysteries of life; perhaps in this book you will find your own light. In this book you will be given the basic ingredients of a recipe for some metaphysical premises, but it will be up to you to make a gourmet meal that will suit your palate. Have the greatest of banquets! Good luck on finding the torch to blaze your way!

The Survival Hypothesis 1

*Science is built up of facts, as a house is built of
stones; but an accumulation of facts is no more a
science than a heap of stones is a house.*
—JULES HENRI POINCARÉ

The Universal Law Simply Stated

Nothing happens by chance, because for every effect there is a cause; therefore, there is purpose and reason as to why everything happens, has happened, or will ever happen.

It is not by magic, circumstance, or random accident that life of some kind must be scattered throughout our known universe, such as on our beloved planet earth.

Conversely, we know that the laws of nature abhor waste and the vacuum that results when a life form is eradicated by disasters to that organism or when cessation comes to certain species, such as ourselves, individually or collectively.

In our case, an unknown created us, nourished us—natural selection or not—and will eventually guide us to our demise in the short or long term.

For what reason or purpose do life forms exist anyway—an accident of random selection or chance? Are human beings merely cogs in the wheel of the vast universe? We know we are composed of atoms and energy, or matter, if you will. Matter is the basic composition of the universe. We don't know as yet, and possibly will never know the reason why life exists, but the suspicion is that the fifteen-billion-year-old universe is not a massive machine that runs forever on its own power. It must have a purpose.

As exciting discoveries continue to occur in physics and astronomy, we are assured that many new hypotheses will be propounded that will begin to join together more pieces in the puzzle that is the universe. For example, it was recently hypothesized that 90 percent of our universe is composed of an invisible dark matter, which then leaves only 10 percent that we are presently able to discern through telescopes, outer space probes, and scientific speculation.

Einstein's brilliant theory of relativity, proven then disproven, depending on the moment, seems to effect and affect our concept of the known universe, and it continues to be the most startling collection of theories held—a conglomeration of speculations, such as of dimensions where there is no absolute time and space. Then we piggyback theories of no solid particles, atomic fission, the big bang theory, chaos theory, continued expansion of the universe, and the rest. These theories add more spice to the cosmic soup of speculation, which will take many years to prove or refute (if it's ever possible).

A Quick Review of Science 101

Let's review some of what we know from science so we have a base from which to explore the assumptions in our universal law stated above.

The first law of thermodynamics states that everything in our universe is comprised of matter, which simply means electromagnetic energy and atoms. Matter is anything that possesses mass and occupies space. It is comprised of atoms that contain nuclei made up of protons and neutrons. This law of physics further states that energy cannot be destroyed or created but only redistributed, that is, changed to other forms of energy.

There are three kinds of matter: solids, liquids, and gases. All matter, including our physical bodies, is mostly empty spaces, with vibrating electrons that make objects appear as solids. Human bodies are made up of solids, liquids, and gases, but we are mainly rigid and hard (atoms close together, or at least they appear to be so). We have a fixed shape and a fixed amount of space due to these atoms. Our lives function in an environment of dense, physical matter of known dimensions.

Currently there are four classified dimensions: length, width, depth, and time. A fifth dimension, gravity, is currently being theorized. The superstring theory propounds that there might be multiple dimensions, resulting in multiple universes instead of a single universe. Perhaps as many as ten dimensions exist. The quantum theory of mechanics, pertaining to this specific area, states that the universe, our universe, is constantly moving and shifting into these alternate dimensions, or realities.

Quantum physics practitioners are investigating and revisiting scientifically held theories and rationale on the mass and unity of the universe. It is an area concerned with the interaction of all matter, with the superstring theory; relative motion; the electromagnetic field of the earth and the universe; as well as time, space, and velocity. It is a reliable premise that these areas of study and other related investigations will continue to revolutionize old and new theories in physics.

This quick study of basic physics is lacking when it attempts to approach the complexities of science, in particular the physics of the universe. The first law of thermodynamics, the nuances of the universe, and quantum physics are difficult for the layman to understand at best. These brief explanations have been approached in order to establish a humble baseline of knowledge for exposure to the possibilities of alternative views of human personality survival. With the complexities of our universe, its function, purpose, and vastness, there is room for divergent viewpoints, especially when so many of us have had glimpses into the otherside.

Two questions surface unanswered from this brief review: Is it possible to reduce *everything* to the level of matter? And what is the *real* nature of time and space (which does affect an afterlife)? Perhaps quantum theory—a remodeling of the universe that also includes study of Extrasensory Perception (ESP) and paranormal events, the sensory and the clairvoyant—will cause a shakeup in the scientific community. Could this new field draw theology and science into a truce?

It is very possible under quantum theories that there might be a parallel universe, which was proposed by early occultists who believed that this is where the afterworld is.

So, What Does This Mean to Us?

- We are composed of the universe's matter.

- The essence of all matter is activity, movement, and interaction; all things are dynamic and in a state of continual motion, flux, and vibration.

- Who or what force put everything in motion, and for what purpose?

- Perhaps all matter has a "mind" of its own.

- Everything is interdependent and interrelated.

- We are one with the universe, its material, its energy, its force, and we, like the universe, do have a purpose as yet unknown; nature does not waste energy.

- When our physical body dies and decomposes, the matter is redistributed.

- Where is our matter redistributed?

- Quantum Mechanics states that our universe is constantly moving into alternate dimensions and realities.

- With as many dimensions as we know of presently, and the others as yet unknown, is there a possibility of a dimension being that "astral plane" of the afterworld?

- There is no absolute in time or space.

- The universe is beyond our total comprehension.

- The unfathomable and vast universe seems to make room for all things and knows nothing of our scientifically imposed structures.

- There is no empirical data on the soul.

- Nothing in science can ever be predicted with one hundred percent accuracy and concrete absoluteness.

The Brain, More Controversy

Now let's turn from physics to another of the most exciting areas of speculation, the brain. The brain is accepted as the seat of power in the human being and other advanced animals. Neurological labels such as amygdala, parietal lobes, somatosensory cortex, and thalamus can be confusing, but, what critical areas of the brain they are! The brain retains memory and controls movement, actions, and communications. It assists with concentration, organizes everything in the body, and spurs thought processing and creative inspiration.

It is felt that internal electrical stimulation, or a lack of impulses from the temporal lobes, can lead to transcendent experiences like visions, hearing voices, and thinking "ethereal" thoughts, supposedly producing Out of Body Events (OBEs), Near Death Experiences (NDEs), and supernatural or spiritual thoughts. Notice I said that it is "felt"; it is very much an unknown. Does the "mind's eye," or mental imagery, overlap with visual perception? Maybe about 40 percent of the workings of the visual cortex (at the back of the brain) are unknown; could this account for visions, perceptions, and perceived psychic phenomena? As you can see, further investigations in the science of the brain will be needed, but for now, much is speculation.

However, we are again met with hypotheses and theories. Simply put, the brain is such a vast and complicated mechanism, a universe unto itself, that scientific logic, research, and current technology will find it difficult to pin down the concrete facts. The magnificent brain is a biological machine that propels movement, and it is an absolutely stunning instrument for gathering and processing information. Some theologians and medical practitioners call the human brain "The House of God on Earth."

There are two theoretical (philosophical) approaches to the brain:

Dualism: The mind is separate from the brain. Thoughts from the brain cannot be measured, weighed, seen, touched, heard, or smelled; these thoughts are the sum total of the human personality (ego), the soul, the storehouse of the total mental experience, separate, although shaped by physical experiences. What is the relationship of mind to matter? Is the mind in existence apart from the body? Rene Descartes, a seventeenth-century French philosopher, said, "I think, therefore I am." Dualism means two: the brain and the mind.

Monism: This approach does not accept the premise that the brain and mind are separate. Monism is strongly supported by the scientific and medical community. The mind and its thoughts are not considered matter in any form. Monism means one, the brain alone.

Much confusion over the brain and its mental functions will continue. The easy retreat is to state that the mind with all of its thoughts is entirely a function of the brain. We do know that the brain's function is governed by electrical impulses and can be measured by EEGs, PET scans, the new FRMI, and so on. Brain waves can be measured in electrical Hertz, or cycles per second. The human brain, like our bodies and everything in the universe is matter. Since it is known that no matter can be destroyed, just redistributed, the question is, then: Where does the mind with its thoughts go when the body's matter is being shifted elsewhere? Thoughts are not wasted, as the universe conserves everything; this question then becomes a true metaphysical headache.

Spiritualists and some other religions across the world believe in an ethereal body, an almost complete replicate of the physical body, that detaches from the physical body at death (NDEs, OBEs temporarily included). The surviving ego (human personality) goes with it into the universe. This energy of the mind, if the personality was/is strong enough, remains intact. The mind-thoughts-soul creates its own reality, and the options of direction commence.

Skeptics and the Acceptance of Finality

The skeptic will unthinkingly accept the scientific rationale because of the vast strides that have been accomplished in techno-materialism. There are, according to the skeptic, good reasons to refute the idea that the universe was created by a great "unseen": "If a God did not exist, then man would have to invent him," is a well-known quote paraphrased from Voltaire.

Skeptics have a tendency either to ignore what they cannot explain or scoff and adopt a single, easy solution that provides instant answers. Primarily, in spite of the possibilities, antisurvivalists consider the thought of personality survival after death as pure delusion and nonsense. How sad indeed, for a closed mind gathers no challenging thoughts.

The school of scientific skeptics propounds that a human being is a DNA-driven machine with a brain comprised of biologic fluids and that the universe is a mathematical equation. Some refute the premise of a purpose for human life with a slap-dash response—that the one, brief, coincidental spark of existence was solely for fulfilling nature's role of procreation of an accidental species.

Let the skeptics remain skeptical, for nothing the survivalists say or do will make any difference. Perhaps as this new century continues to make great inroads into all facets of life, and in particular when new revelations about death and the survival of the human personality become known, they will then find their way.

Summary

The Survival Hypothesis—that life does not end when death takes over—can be hotly debated, seemingly forever. Fundamental arguments over what the great universal truth is and what illusion is will continue to crop up. Do we deceive ourselves into believing that paranormal events transpire? Do they seem to occur only because we want them to occur? Does our stunning advance in technology prove that misguided beliefs in the supernatural are a fraud? After all, these are modern times.

We do know that recent advances being made in parapsychology and paranormal studies are relevant, but many are sadly lacking in scientific laboratory structure and organization. Science is materialistic, mechanistic, technology-driven, and fundamentally antispiritual. It refuses to consider anything that cannot be lab-analyzed, formulated, measured, classified, weighed, and reduced to a chemical, physical, or biological formula. Nevertheless, hundreds of thousands of paranormal cases across the world, some quasi-documented, a few even observed under the most stringent of circumstances, still indicate that we continue to have NDEs, OBEs, visions, intuitions, and encounters with the deceased. It is very appropriate in this new millennium that we continue to investigate the limitless universe, make tremendous breakthroughs in medicine, and achieve stunning advances in technology—and that we should now attempt to discover the purpose of our existence and the last frontier—death and survival. With the brainpower and technological resources available, science, theology, and parapsychology can now join together to determine what is perhaps the greatest final exploration.

Anyone seeing the magnificent pictures from the numerous space exploration programs, especially those received from the Mariner 9 probe, the Viking 2 project, the Mars Global Surveyor, and the Voyager and Hubble space telescopes, cannot help but be overwhelmed, awed, and washed in humility. The tag line is this: We are the stuff that this vast universe is made of. We are the same substance of every star, comet, cosmic dust particle, body of water, plant, insect, animal, building, table, and chair! And like this vast universe we are part of, we are also able to switch into another form of energy. We have an additional universe (or universes) to be absorbed into when our energy configuration changes from decay to "rebirth." With great elation we should come to the realization that we are all part of the great cosmic puzzle.

As stated in our universal law at the beginning of this chapter, nothing happens by chance, because for every effect there is a cause; therefore, there is purpose and reason as to why everything happens, has happened, or will ever happen. Our life and death are interconnected because the universe does not make mistakes. Understanding and working in and under this law, in a mental, physical, emotional, psychical, and spiritual state can bring peace of mind, happiness, prosperity, and good health. Knowing the higher purpose of our lives and how everything fits together—and being able to separate fact from fiction—this is what it comes down to.

Knowledge of the natural laws of the universe and of our very physical existence will not come like a thunderbolt from the heavens, and surely we can't tap into all truths, but we can realize the universe and its laws are the supreme governing override. Neither science nor metaphysics can ever provide all of the answers, but perhaps if we put them together we can approach the truth at last.

Mediums realize that there are no pat answers to the questions of death, the next world, and reincarnation. They see, listen, and talk to the departed without the aid of science, medicine, technology, or theology; they do know, however, that the mystery of life and the nature of the universe is a package containing sweet and sad things, all wrapped in the excitement of anticipated discovery.

The great tragedy of Science—
the slaying of a beautiful hypothesis by an ugly fact
—THOMAS H. HUXLEY

Mugged by Death 2

I am counting the days until the final holiday
—FREDERIC W. H. MYERS

Death awaits us all. Indeed, the old saying "we are born to die" lurks in the shadows of our minds. A callow statement like "Others wait while we vacate our parking space" even holds some truth. The fact that we are self-important, ego-driven beings is not a demeaning statement, because it is relevant. When we come face-to-face with our mortality and are not yet ready for the big departure, will we be able to let go of the anger, hurt, prostrations of grief, and of course, our possessions? Obviously we must, ready or not.

Life can be compared to being on a cruise ship that docks at several exotic ports, when suddenly the voyage becomes interrupted and the passengers are inconvenienced. Death will cease our earthly joys, misery, and woes. Many would even prefer to keep their miseries instead of facing the unknown. It is very difficult, almost close too impossible to remove the fear of death.

Death can only watch and wait, but in the end it greets us all. So why are we surprised when it intrudes in our lives like a thief in the night? We know well that it is the scheme for all living things. These thoughts are not sufficient to comfort us when we lose loved ones, yet somehow we gain strength and resilience to continue with what remains of our lives. Eventually we even pursue happiness and a degree of contentment in spite of ourselves; it seems to be the way of the human condition.

Death or Survival?

According to science, death is the total cessation of life processes that occurs in living organisms such as ourselves; there is even a check-off list for the death of the human being by the medical professional:

- Absence of pulse and heart beat

- Absence of respiration

- Absence of oxygen in the blood

- Absence of a functioning brainstem

The scientific rationale is negatively weighed against the survival of the human personality after clinical death. The chances of soul survival are summarily dismissed by members of the scientific community, couched in such phrases as: "totally unscientific," or "not feasible." However, there was a time in the Western world, for hundreds of years, when what passed as science was deeply rooted in astrology, alchemy, theology, and philosophy (metaphysics). The Roman Catholic church at this time was the sole authority in the Western world; it had the power to make a person a living dead man through excommunication, could burn people at the stake for various infractions, controlled money and property, armies, and kingdoms. The church regulated all doctrines, thoughts, music, art, literature, and higher learning, resulting in little advancement, originality, or scientific experimentation. Many brilliant thinkers and scientists, such as Copernicus, Galileo, Kepler, and Leonardo da Vinci were restrained by the theology of the day. With the Protestant Reformation and the collapse of singular church control, science loosened its restraints and ran—no, galloped—away from the confusion.

The rift between science and theology lasted for additional hundreds of years. Yet in the Islamic world, these two disciplines enjoyed a fairly good marriage, and in the Far East, science and medicine had its origins in religions and various theologies. Today, the Western world mandates the split of religion and science, with science continuing to make magnificent discoveries and innovations.

Discoveries in science and medicine have exploded. Inventions and innovations have revolutionized the way the world lives. Those third world countries that have fallen behind the techno-materialistic revolution will eventually be "rediscovered" as the next consumer. In the meantime their theologies and customs seem to hold them together, loosely or with an iron grip. Materialism is here to stay and flourish, with scientific discovery and innovation continuing to push the envelope.

Since science is not concerned with theology, afterlife investigations are shunted to the side, ignored and spurned. After all, what is scientific about soul survival anyway? What machine can be built that starts life over again, or that probes or explores the afterlife?

Nonetheless, citizens of the world continue to ask the age-old questions that science and medicine refuse to answer. Is the purpose of the universe-earth-plane existence to play out one's role with the circumstances that have been given—and without question? Can it really be believed that there is no magnificent scheme or design for a life? Is there no reason or purpose other than breathing, breeding, working, and consuming? These questions are important to many because it is felt that human lives *do* fit into the universe's grand scheme, and that science—since it has explored other confounding mysteries—can solve the greatest mystery of all.

On page 12 you will find a chart that contrasts death to the survival of the human personality (soul, life force, or spirit).

Options at Death

When we get mugged by death, the natural occurrence of our species, we are taken to the next great adventure. Some people (many millions, actually) in several world cultures and religions believe in reincarnation. Why not? Remember that we, as free souls, not knowing everything that the universe has in store for us, can create this option. Reentry over and over again into this life, until the soul or ego feels that it will get it right after a few more trials, is a possibility for many people. We all have options at our death. Of course, these personal options are organized and listed here, not in mandatory order, but mainly to give you some idea of the choices you can make when you commence the passing over process, especially if you pray, meditate, and have *belief!*

DEATH

We cannot circumvent death by goodness, piety, miraculous cures, pleas, and wealth.

Death is the total and permanent end of all vital functions of any living organism.

In the middle of our lives we draw closer to death.

Death can strike without warning, and usually does.

The anxiety about death is not knowing what comes next.

Death is the permanent annihilation of our physical shell.

We are born to die.

Death is the separation of the material and the immaterial.

Death is a complete change of condition.

Death is not the big sleep.

What we seed in life, we harvest later; it is always time to weed, prepare the soil, and plant—crop rotation can always be done for a reinstatement of life.

Necrophobia is the fear of death and of dead things.

Thanatophobia is the fear of death.

Physical death is the absence of pulse and heartbeat; also absence of respiration, oxygen in blood, and absence of a functioning brainstem.

SURVIVAL

The soul, as the mind, contains memories, consciousness, thoughts, actions, desires, emotions, and experiences.

The soul is energy.

Our personal salvation is soul survival and soul release—transcending death.

As we leave our physical body, our etheric (astral) body (soul) becomes our vehicle of transportation to the otherside.

The soul is mind over matter.

The soul is our spirit and life force.

Confused humans have confused souls.

The soul carries goodness, guilt, and bad deeds like baggage, to the afterlife.

The soul weighs nothing.

There is absolutely no proof that the soul does not exist; paranormal occurrences prove that it does.

The soul is synonymous with self (ego) or mind.

Does the soul preexist the body it's in?

Is our soul powerful enough to reassemble or stay intact?

Karma is the accrual of negative or positive deeds and vibrations.

Option A: The soul of the individual is so strong that it holds its life force (energy) together for the astral planes of the afterworld; this requires a strong belief in an afterlife by the individual.

Option B: The deceased individual refuses to depart for the new life and instead stays on the earth plane for various reasons; the person is said to become earth-bound.

Option C: The soul fragments (energy disperses) due to lack of knowledge, desire, belief, or strength, or it is passive, thereby joining the matter of the universe. The personality is lost.

Option D: The soul's life force goes to the otherside and eventually reenters the earth plane at the conception of a new life or embryo; the reincarnation process commences.

Our universe is a great accepting entity, based on what we know, *and* what we don't know. Science and materialism hold some clues to our present existence, but offer few facts for our future existence.

The Near Death Experience (NDE)

The Near Death Experience is an inky black to a brilliant light experience in which the individual undergoes movement through some sort of tunnel, meeting another bright light. This seems to be a common experience and happens regardless of religion, belief, gender, education, race, or social status. During this process, relatives, spirits, guides, angels and sometimes a Godlike presence greet the nearly deceased. Generally, the individual has a feeling of euphoria, although some negative encounters have also occurred. It seems that most who experience NDE do not want to come back to this life, and decided changes of personality occur, resulting in positive attitudes, morality, and a strong state of inner peace. Regardless of whether the individual was clinically dead or in a state of temporary coma, many who undergo this predeath or death trauma believe in what happened to them, and many have wonderful stories to relate.

Everything concerning the Near Death Experience appears to be explained away by the scientific and medical establishment. Medical researchers have concluded that hypoxia, or a lack of oxygen to the brain, and strong endorphin release coupled with heavy medication are the explanations for this phenomenon. But it again must be restated that so little information is available concerning the experiences of death and the survival of the personality that little empirical proof can be offered one way or another.

Science, directly or indirectly, waffles around the core principle that we might be physically one with the universe—and thus could actually have a purpose and a reason for being here. But it does little good to solicit approval from science about the intangible and the unseen, because, as a subject of study, it currently is not open for debate. The umbrella of rational scientific reasoning departs when debate on the survival of personality is mentioned. Yet if the dreamers and explorers of the world had not overcome barriers to experimentation and innovation, then nothing would have been accomplished in mankind's short history in science, not to mention medicine, agriculture, mathematics, art and music, philosophy, astronomy, social structure, government, justice, and military science.

Experiences with the Otherside

It is difficult to speculate on what the final outcome of death really means, especially when, as we revel in the now and experience the sweetness of this glorious life, suddenly somebody comes along with confusing ideas of supernatural experiences, and the safe and reliable becomes out of whack. It can be unnerving when contact with the otherside is made through seeing into that world or in meeting representatives of that invisible realm, and without any comforting explanations being given. On the other hand, our yearning for another life after this one is undeniable, and faith, belief, and hope can't answer all of our questions unless they are bolstered by personal experiences. Following are some experiences that I hope will shed some light on the world beyond this one.

There are more things in heaven and earth, Horatio,
than are dreamt of in your philosophy.
—WILLIAM SHAKESPEARE, *HAMLET*

A Personal Survival Question Answered

On a recent vacation in New Orleans, Louisiana, my wife, friends, and I were on a walking tour of the city's beautiful Garden District. The tour included Cemetery Number One, which is one of New Orleans's oldest cemeteries.

The crumbling tombs, crypts, and fanciful statuary are almost hidden under numerous lush, spreading trees, some letting little sunlight through, and that day in November, the rain clouds held the sun to a minimum light. It was an easy day of walking despite the high humidity.

As the tour group progressed through the graveled cemetery avenues, I walked considerably behind the group in order to take pictures. Being left behind, I studied the inscriptions on many of the tombs. Then my side vision caught movement. I turned to my left and to the back. There, approximately thirty yards away, I saw a small group of people in the sun-flecked shadows under a small grove of trees. There were about ten "people" in number—children to adults, dressed in gray-colored robes (shrouds?) or nightgowns. Their hair varied in color from blond to black. Their faces were fuzzy and out of focus in the shadows, but I could tell they were deathly pale.

I knew immediately what they were and was so excited I stopped to take further pictures. Some of them, especially a tall woman with two young children, waved at me. I moved toward them slowly and was within approximately twenty yards when they seemed to dissolve—feet first, all the way up to the tops of their heads. In my excited state I took a rapid sequence of pictures.

Later, at an ice-cream parlor across from the cemetery, I could barely contain my excitement over the proof that was contained in my camera. The tour guide, a retired professor from a local university, drew me aside as we were leaving the parlor and said in a soft drawl, "Get their pictures?" Disappointedly, after the film was developed, I found I only had pictures of tombs and crypts, not even a telltale hint of ghostly streaks or shadows.

I mention this experience to emphasize that unexplained things do occur, especially when one is receptive and open. This brief encounter reinforced my belief in another life—and I do know what I saw, not what I think I saw, and again I had another personal reaffirmation that we continue after physical death.

And Another One

On that same trip to New Orleans, we were lodged in a beautiful and very old (1700s), time-share in the French Quarter. While there for a few days, I strongly felt there were more people inhabiting our suite of rooms than our party. My face, nose, ears, and hair in particular felt like something was caressing them. Being a sensitive, or medium, I knew we were their guests.

I had a fitful sleep that night and awoke abruptly, strongly sensing a young male soldier standing next to my bed. I don't remember seeing his "physical" presence, being half-awake, but I knew he was not a malevolent spirit, only a sad one. Since I didn't feel in any danger I went back to sleep.

The next morning on the wharf, we stopped at a tourist booth to gather information of sites to visit and to book several tours. I talked to the lady at the booth, and the conversation eventually came around to where we were staying. Her eyes grew large as quarters when she told me in a hushed voice that she and her husband used to own the place we were staying at. They had sold it because ghosts had "bothered" their children. It seems the building was once a veteran's hospital in the late 1700s or early 1800s. Men had died there, some having been buried on the grounds at one time. Unfortunately she was too busy to go into ghost stories; however, I could tell from her eyes that she could have described some rather exciting spirit happenings.

On that same trip we toured several magnificent plantation homes on the Mississippi River. Constant vibrations almost overpowered me while touring those homes; for the most part they seemed filled with sadness—it happens in homes where generations of people have lived. It would have been very interesting to spend a night or two in some of those old, stately homes just to see what could have been "absorbed."

I air these impressions in order to emphasize that we live an unusual life in an unusual universe; nothing is truly as it seems on the surface. You can have ironclad logic to guide you and lead you through life, but when the ground rules collapse, a new equation is added.

For skeptics who have no belief at all concerning survival after death, perhaps rigid empiricism, the philosophy of the Stoics, which allows no wiggle room for reevaluation, would be most suitable.

The Newspaper Boy

As a young newspaper boy of fourteen, my route included an old mansion district in the Capitol Hill area of Denver. Numerous turn-of-the-century mansions had been converted into cheap apartments, with most of the occupants being elderly people. I would drop off several morning newspapers in the lobby of these converted mansions and collect at the end of each month.

One of the oldest and grandest of these mansions had several subscribers that were particularly generous with tips, even though I did nothing exceptional in delivering the newspaper. One morning while picking up my newspapers from the route manager, the manager asked why I continued to deliver papers to this particular residence since it was scheduled to be demolished, and the residents had left some time ago.

I was very confused since I had collected from six units the previous week. We agreed to meet at the mansion after I was through delivering the rest of the route. When we arrived, the door to the lobby was open but the rest of the house was boarded up here and there, and in the lobby, stacks of newspapers were on the floor and not on the credenza near the front door where I usually put them. The lobby was empty and dirty, and after going through two apartments on the main floor, we found no furniture!

I knew I had talked to them, seen them, and collected money from them, but nobody was in the mansion and obviously hadn't been for some time—the thick dust didn't lie. The route manager said he had heard the property was supposedly haunted and that a law firm that had almost purchased the property months ago for law offices decided not to buy after hearing of several ghostly complaints from the contractors.

I still have an unusual oversized dollar bill from the 1920s given to me as a tip. I have little doubt that I had entered into a haunted situation (a time warp?) and only wish I had been aware enough to savor the experience and to learn from the deceased.

A Friend's Experience

M., one of my wife's close friends, has a degenerative eye disease that drove her to see an eye specialist. The doctor's prognosis was not very encouraging and M. went into the lady's restroom to be alone with the bad news. She was so overcome with the negative news that she broke down and cried, then suddenly noticed a brilliant orange glow in the restroom drawing toward her.

She heard a very familiar voice—her deceased mother's, which said, "M., don't be upset, everything will be OK." She felt her mother's warm hands on her and experienced a surge of energy. After a couple of minutes, the light dissipated. M. is one of those people who live with extreme logic and little panic, and who usually question most things. She has changed somewhat in supernatural beliefs now, and her eye problem is in an arrested state at this writing. She still relishes her departed mother's visit.

A Scientist's Story

J. is a research toxicologist working at a state university who believes strongly in scientific rationale and logic. She had been very close to her brother-in-law. One day, she relates, she felt exceptionally distracted and depressed for no known reason while conducting lab experiments. Later that night, she received a telephone call from her sister in Virginia, informing her that the young, athletic brother-in-law had suddenly died from a heart attack that very day. The following evening, her brother-in-law appeared to J., discussed some private matters, then disappeared.

Close to this event, J.'s father also passed away and has appeared to her on several occasions. J. is still a very hard-nosed scientist, but has left open the options on life after death.

Telephone Calls

My mother and I were estranged for several years due to some ugly family scraps in the past. She lived a considerable distance away, in Arkansas, and we never saw each other, telephoned, or wrote. One night, I assume in my usual deep sleep, she telephoned me in my dreams. I recognized her voice in spite of heavy static. Her voice was faint, but I could discern that she was upset, and I couldn't make out what she was trying to tell me. I abruptly awakened, drenched in the sweat of guilt.

The next morning I told my wife about the strange dream, but it was quickly forgotten through the day's activities. That night she again called me in my dream, and this time I was able to make out an apology for our ridiculous separation. Before I could respond we were disconnected. Again I told my wife about the strange dream. I even thought about calling my mother but was afraid of being rebuffed.

The next day, which was a Sunday, my uncle called to tell me that he had just learned from my step-father that my mother had passed away two days prior!

What's not to be believed? Supernatural experiences happen to all of us in our lifetimes, yet the majority of us don't make a connection; we forget, push aside, can't remember, don't want to remember, or chalk up the encounter as ridiculous and silly. We all try to avoid being put down as "kooks."

The purpose of the vignettes laced throughout this book serve to illustrate the premise that supernatural events can and do happen. We all eventually get mugged by death, and these events can offer some hope that we "live" again. After my first book was published, I received several telephone calls from nurses who worked in hospices. They believed in NDEs and other paranormal events because their dying patients informed them of experiences that had occurred. My daughter, who works in the medical profession, shared several discussions with me she had had with doctors, some believing in life after death, and others strongly in NDEs. Medical practitioners are very much afraid of breaking from the mold because of the fear of being branded as unprofessional and strange by colleagues and patients.

A Question of Faith

I know not all people of a metaphysical bent work in the religious or unworldly professions, but I was rather taken aback by a statement from a crime scene investigator and assistant to the county coroner— scientific and heavy with credentials—that reaffirms that fact. When she was asked how she dealt with death and the volume of bodies she examined, she stated bluntly that when she looked at the corpse she knew it was only a shell—"the soul is long gone, you know, and when I start an examination I always wish them Godspeed to the next place—in the event they are still hanging around."

It is a question of faith, and faith can be found in all walks of life. Here is a kind of creed that might be common to all who believe:

- The universe did not commence by accident.

- Life, in all forms, did not just happen.

- There are no absolutes.

- We humans are spiritual beings in a material existence.

- Events in all things are bound up in synchronicity; there is a reason for every "accident" and all are interrelated and connected.

- Life is the schoolhouse for spiritual preparation and continuation in the afterlife.

- We create our own reality with our thoughts.

What Mediums Believe

And here are a set of beliefs specific to mediums:

- There is life after death.

- The Invisible World of spirit is a real place.

- It's hard for us, and some spirits, to release the world of materialism.

- Spirit guides and guardian angels are with us from birth to death.

- Fear and skepticism builds a wall that cuts us off from spirit contact.

- LOVE is the essential and greatest force of this life and the next one.

- We are granted a contract at conception or birth with the universe for our lives. This contract is NOT to be taken lightly or abused.

- If you've done "minor" or negative things to yourself and others, pray; if a lot of negative things, continue to pray, apologize, and CHANGE; do evil here, you will yourself into evil, and there are consequences.

- Sincere and frequent meditation can produce and enhance the abilities of clairvoyance, clairaudience, and clairsentience.

- Anger, hatred, lust, and greed destroy positive energy.

- Dreams are an excellent catalyst for intuition, visions, spirit messages, and spirit visits.

- Personality survival after death is proven by spirit messages, paranormal occurrences, NDEs, and apparitions.

- Negative or positive Karma is accrued by nations, politicians, businesses, institutions, and individuals; a time always comes for a payoff, plus or minus.

What Is a Medium? 3

All is illusion;
I do not know whether I am a man dreaming I am a butterfly
or if I am a butterfly dreaming I am a man.
—ATTRIBUTED TO CHUANG-TZU, TAOIST POET (220 B.C.)

A Short History of Mediumship

Mediumship, the art of spirit communication, has been with us since early man. Spiritual contact appears in every culture and civilization and in some form in most religions. Many holy books in the faiths of the world allude to it or cite instances of it. And prophets and disciples of those theologies have used it for visions and guidance, even in today's hurry-up world.

Mediumship and Spiritualism spring from roots deep in history, but some modern practices began to evolve in the early eighteenth century. A brilliant Swedish scientist and mystic, Emanuel Swedenborg, would slip into a deep trancelike state and communicate with spirits and angels from the otherside. The astounding messages and prophecies he received were documented and were mainly in the context of religious and practical matters—accurate and to the point. Ministers of Sweden, as well as scientists and the royal family, were guided by messages and readings Swedenborg received from the otherside.

Later in the eighteenth century, Franz Mesmer, an Austrian physician, formally discovered the hypnosis method and found that a hypnotic trance brought visions and spirit communications, as well as self-healing. His diagnosis and treatment of disease through hypnosis was also a benefit of this "mesmeric" trance, and this method of hypnotic trance became part of spiritual healing in the 1800s. He also introduced the idea that magnets could cure disabilities and illness, a controversy that still overshadows his hypnosis theories.

Modern-day mediumship as we know it commenced with the Fox sisters of Hydesville, New York, in 1848, when these young women heard raps and noises from a supposedly murdered salesman buried in their basement. This incident, fraudulent or not—there is much conjecture over this matter—evolved eventually into the birth of a semi-Christian religious faith called Spiritualism, which quickly spread throughout North America, South America, Europe, and Asia. It's been estimated that more than ten million Americans in the nineteenth century claimed to be Spiritualists, attending hundreds of Spiritualist churches, and that well over 22,000 self-proclaimed mediums handled the crowds in America alone.

Table tipping by spirit forces became enormous entertainment in salons and parties throughout Europe and evolved into formal spirit communication gatherings—the séance (French for "sitting"). In the séance sessions, a group of like-minded believers and the curious sat around a table, holding or touching each others hands for positive energy vibrations, while a selected medium (the spirit world go-between) would direct or answer questions to and from the spirit world.

Many famous and talented individuals with the gift believed and participated in séances, and while rampant fraud discredited some mediums and séances, the popularity of these sittings continued unabated.

Laws were passed in several European countries as well as a handful of American states to curtail suspected fraud under the infamous "Witchcraft Laws." Donation gifts or "love" offerings instead of fees seemed to skirt the laws in some instances. Fraud was committed by elaborate stage crafting, gathering personal information before the séance was held, optical illusions, trapdoors, magic tricks, all running the gamut of the ridiculous.

Despite hints of outright fraud, generals, statesmen, inventors, scientists, prime ministers, even an American president and members of royal families, including several kings and queens, continued attending sessions, some following to the letter what the spirits told the trance medium. The séance as a formal spirit communication method was incorporated into several cults and religions—in meditation, prophecy, healing, and vision methods still used to this day. Plays, novels, poems, and short stories incorporated mediums and the séance as a central storyline and plot. Of course, everyone today is familiar with European and American movies that weave the séance into the main plot.

Several above-board societies were founded for scientific and psychical research in the late 1800s, with numerous and eminent scientists, parapsychologists, public officials, and academicians banding together to investigate alleged paranormal events; some of these continue to the present. Of the many thousands of claims scientifically investigated, a number of these cases, scrutinized under the most stringent conditions, were blessed with authenticity—and still received with skepticism. Sadly, the results of most of these now historical findings lay buried in dusty library stacks and archives, perhaps never to be read again. Psychical research institutes and a few, brave universities with paranormal research facilities continue to survive with limited funding.

During and after World War I, especially in Europe, séances, and mediums in general, were extremely popular, particularly among the many thousands of parents and loved ones who had lost their young men in the horrific carnage of that war.

In the 1920s an American magician and illusionist, the great Harry Houdini, made it his life's work to discredit mediums and the séance, while his sometime friend, Sir Arthur Conan Doyle, attempted to prove the validity of spirit communications. In the case of Doyle, a feeding frenzy of ridicule by the worldwide press and journals occurred, hounding this brave and outspoken man to his grave in the early 1930s. Sadly, it seems almost impossible to state your beliefs to the world if you believe in the paranormal, and this is what happened to the brilliant creator of Sherlock Holmes.

Practitioners of Spiritualism, especially in Brazil and the United Kingdom, continue to thrive. The historical weave of great mediums such as D. D. Home, Leona Piper, Mrs. Garrett, and others gave proof that spirit communications through mediums via the séance was a possible and reliable avenue for communicating with the deceased.

Today there are Spiritualist towns in the United States where residents conduct the arts of prophecy, healing, and mediumship.

Mediums and psychics living in Lily Dale, New York, and Cassadega, Florida, conduct lectures, readings, study sessions, and worship services for residents and numerous visitors.

What Is a Medium?

A medium is a focused individual who believes strongly in life after death and in spirit communication. Mediums do not believe in constraints imposed by science, theology, or in thinking within the box. The medium with years of practice and skill is contacted by or contacts the deceased. The interchange of these messages are personal, many times to the point, and sometimes rather vague—a big picture versus little picture, or vice versa—and the reading often seems to fit situations in the days or months ahead.

The Mystic

Some confusion results when the term mediumship is used because mediums, like mystics, are often enigmatic and involved with occult practices. Comparisons of the mystic and medium are often intertwined; however, there are numerous differences, even though the mystic in our society and culture also looks beyond traditional reality.

Unlike mediums, mystics are usually oblivious to the problems of self, others, society, and the world in general. Spiritual enlightenment is their focus, and retreat and withdrawal for periods of time appear to charge their batteries. Most times they leave material possessions behind while they search, sometimes even living like hermits in seclusion while building their own private reality.

Many famous individuals throughout world history have indulged their egos in the wash of the mystic. Jesus, Mohammed, Joan of Arc, the Buddha, many biblical prophets, Roman Catholic saints, Zen masters, various gurus, and of course, the mythical (?) magician, Merlin. Of course, some of these had mediumistic abilities, but for our purpose they are not to be considered modern-day mediums.

Why Mediumship?

Before we go into the medium's craft, we need to explain the "why." A person is born to live, fulfill his or her life as much as possible, then cross over. While a person slugs out a living in the trenches, hopefully with joy and self-actualization, they become older as the natural progression continues before the inevitable happens: "Where did the time go?"

In far too many countries and societies of the world, fulfillment does not allow the full measure of joy and optimism in life. Disease, wars, politics, prostitution and drugs, slavery, lack of decent water and food, back-breaking work, all terminate a person's existence prematurely. For some, the only hope for a better existence is death and the promise of a better world through some sort of heaven or paradise— maybe even through a later retry by reincarnation. Theology, through religious declarations and holy book interpretations offer the promise of a better world later. But doubt still surfaces, especially in individuals who question the existence of an afterlife. For those who are better off, this modern world of science and technology, filled with things we can actually touch, feel, hear, taste, and use, makes it hard to propose that there exists a glorious possibility that we can move on to another world, an invisible one, no less. It becomes problematic to explain the concept of how it's possible to pass over without the physical body. After all, aren't computers, machines, automobiles, thrown into landfills or crushers when broken or used up? Everything can be trashed, then why not us? What makes us so special anyway? If something as fragile and perfect as our God-given body heads for a hole in the ground or a crematorium when it's worn out, perhaps broken like a technological toy, then isn't everything disposable? How could a spirit force of some kind be lodged in our brain then freed in a fuzzy, metaphysical transition?

It is difficult at best for the vast majority of us to take a leap of faith into a spiritual, transitional conception from the materialistic hard copy of what we know, because this material world has been our only reality. Thoughts of personal immortality simply do not compute for the majority of people in the twenty-first century. Aging Baby Boomers and their progeny know that modern medicine and science cannot prolong human life indefinitely, that diet, exercise, and money will not stay the shadow that waits for them. Some "modern miracles" certainly can prolong and even add to the quality of living, but not forever.

The medium, through contact with the invisible world, attempts to furnish proof of survival, insight, and alleviation of these fears of total oblivion and termination. Our spirit, essence, or soul lives long after our physical death. No words or thoughts in any language can fully express or explain the incredible journey that we shall undertake. How, then, can a medium, mystic, or theologian convey the facts of a totally new world of existence? In the next section we will explore what methods mediums use to illuminate the spirit world.

What Does a Medium Do?

There are two types of mediums that have traditionally specialized in spirit contact:

Mental: Most common in mediumship; communication comes through the mind. The medium acts like a two-way radio receiver or a telephone while in a deep or semideep trance and leads séance sessions.

Physical: This now almost historical form of mediumship produces floating objects, levitation, and a whitish substance called ectoplasm from body orifices that become the hands, head, or bodies of the deceased. They are able to manifest spirits during the séance for participants to see and talk with.

Most mediums can have several special abilities in:

Clairvoyance: (clear seeing) in which the medium "sees" spirits and events

Clairaudience: (clear hearing) when the medium hears departed spirits

Clairsentience: (clear sensing) sensing the presence of spirits, events, and past events; living individuals and spirits can leave an imprint on a room or place that can be felt in the present (energy scars)

Mediums can have all three abilities, and when the vibrations are optimum in the surrounding environment, especially during a séance where all the participants are positive and like-minded, readings can occur.

Now, it must be said that some confusion results in combining other gifted spirit communicators.

Psychic: Has the ability to "feel" and see events—past, present, and future—by reading tarot and playing cards, use of astrology, reading palms, crystal ball gazing, or reading tea leaves. Psychics usually do not specialize in deceased communications. They can be very good at picking up thoughts and activities of living individuals. Some use no tools, just their minds.

Channelers: Communicates with entities in the universe. Advice and guidance is given through the channeler to the requester in such matters as finance and love, and advice from a universal entity. Channeling is perhaps the oldest psychic art known to mankind.

A true medium will attempt to combine the abilities of clairvoyance, clairaudience, and clairsentience, especially during a séance, personal reading, or "soul rescue." The best communication with a deceased individual occurs with spirits who have been deceased no longer than twenty earth years, the strongest being with those deceased less than five years.

Mediums can be excellent receivers and conductors for prophecy, healing, reading auras (to determine physical and emotional health), scrying (future gazing through mirrors, water, and candles—think Nostradamus), and psychometry (readings from personal objects). Some mediums are able to produce apparitions and objects (apports) from the otherside. An enormous amount of energy and mind control is involved, and gender does seem to make a difference in utilizing these abilities, women usually being more successful. As the medium gets older the use of these gifts tends to weaken somewhat due to the enormous amount of stamina, focus, and energy that is required.

A Typical "Old Fashioned" Séance

A séance is a gathering of a medium and participants for the express purpose of communicating with the departed. The séance can be a one-on-one session for readings or with as many as six to eight like-minded individuals. Like-minded individuals emit positive energy vibrations that can translate into a successful sitting with optimum results. A skeptical person or two will not destroy a productive reading, but why bother with a hardnosed, negative-energy-emitting person in the first place?

The séance is for two-way communication and requires a maximum amount of positive energy flow. The sitters are not assembled to prove anything to anyone, as some might think. Indeed, this author was invited to appear on a local radio talk show with the express purpose of receiving lottery numbers from the otherside during a studio séance session. I'm afraid the station's personality was miffed when I declined to do so. The departed have no more idea what lottery numbers will be drawn than we do. Even if they did, it would've been an abuse of energy and spirit time; spirits do not care about the lottery.

I once did a New York morning radio talk show with the express purpose of explaining the séance and spirit world. Instead, I got calls from people who wanted to know about financial and love life matters. I won't do this again because the séance's purpose is not for psychic readings and instant gratification over the telephone, unlike some psychic hot lines. The séance is, or should be, used for grief alleviation, knowledge and comfort, and two-way communication, not for hot showbiz topics.

It is a commonly held fallacy that formal Spiritualistic séance sessions are passé, an archaic vehicle left over from the past, somehow quaint and Hollywood, and that channeling and psychics have taken over because of lucrative book deals and television spots. Not true. The séance and real mediums are at work as you are reading this book. Perhaps séances and bona fide mediums are fewer in numbers now, some worn around the edges, so to speak, but the craft continues and will last as it has for generations. No doubt when scientific advancement is eventually made through paranormal studies and research, the validity and craft sophistication of the trance medium and séance will be revealed and perhaps even flourish again.

Who has need of a medium or séance? Ask the people who have had the intense sorrow of losing loved ones. Some might even seek personal counseling to alleviate the fear of death. A séance offers a private, in-depth, nondramatic, unhurried solution to these concerns. It can answer questions such as: "What is it like to be dead?" "What is it like over there?" "Will I ever see a certain person again?" Innocuous questions on the surface perhaps, but they still require answers, and a private reading can offer enough comfort and relief to make it through a day, a month, or the years ahead.

Recently I conducted a weekly evening séance study circle for a month at a spiritual science church I attend. The course went into the formal aspects of how to conduct the student's own study circle, ritual, and séance. I commenced with the maximum number of eight students and ended with three students. The feedback was positive, but I couldn't understand why students were dropping out of class—I was paranoid until I talked to several of the students; my findings were not a shocking revelation. It is difficult to hold in-depth study techniques, meditation exercises, and step-by-step ritual activities with students who are mesmerized by the warp speed of our daily lives. Quick answers and solutions are what drive our society. We are a now, lets-get-with-it culture. However, learning and leading a séance is like the aging of a fine wine in a cask: it can't be hurried; the taste and aroma will render proof of quality.

Séance Etiquette and Session Concerns

For a séance to be successful it is best that certain conditions be met.

- Use a private room (with a feeling of good vibrations) and keep the door closed.

- Disconnect the telephone; cell phones and pagers must be turned off.

- Light should be kept soft; have two white candles ready to be lit during the séance.

- Faint instrumental music in the background for white noise if desired; this will help keep unwanted noises from disturbing the sitters.

- Flowers with a light fragrance will enhance the mood.

- Have comfortable chairs—if possible, situated around a round sturdy table.

- Provide cool water with enough glasses for everyone; do not use ice, as this will create noise.

- Have a dish of hard candy for energy.

- No alcohol or drugs (prior to, or during the sitting) should be permitted.

- Set up a tape recorder with enough blank tapes so you can replay readings (if all parties agree).

- Bad and startling news is best withheld until a follow-up or private reading is agreed upon.

- Everything that occurs in a sitting must remain private.

The Full Ritual: For Strong Communication Channels

Begin with introductions of the participants with brief declarations of what they would like to achieve in the sitting and why they are attending the session.

Then the participants stand for the Cleaning of the Aura, in which they briefly rub the palms of their hands together until they feel the heat from the friction. They each then move their hands over and around their head—not touching head or neck. When they feel they have "cleaned" their aura of negative vibrations, they vigorously shake their hands loose of the negative material. Repeat at least twice or until everyone feels confident that their aura has been cleansed. Now, everyone, still standing, joins hands (for a Circle of Energy), while the medium or chosen medium lights two white candles with a wooden kitchen match. Note: candles appear to attract spirits and are used as a purifying agent. The medium, while lighting the candle will say:

> "Spirits above,
> Spirits below,
> Spirits to the North,
> Spirits to the South,
> Spirits to the East,
> Spirits to the West,
> Please attend us and let us see."

Or, as an Alternative Invocation:

> "We bring the cosmic forces into our bodies,
> asking for the protection of the White Light,
> please bring us strength and guidance."

Everyone is then seated around the table, or in chairs arranged in a circle; if seated at a table the participants continue to hold hands or touch hands until the medium commences the session. All persons sit straight up in their chair—spine straight, feet flat on the floor, with eyes closed to become relaxed, all the while breathing in through the nose, and softly exhaling through the mouth. Rhythmic breathing is done until the sitters feel at ease and a little light-headed. The sitters attempt to clear their minds by imagining a blank, white movie screen.

The medium will continue to ask everyone to clear his or her mind while breathing in and expelling their breath, until he or she feels everyone is relaxed. On cue from the medium, everyone will mentally picture a cloud of white, protective light enveloping their entire body, from the floor to the top of their head. They will then be surrounded by the divine, or God's protection—safe from any unwanted entity.

With the White Light of protection enveloping the sitters, the medium will ask who would like to make contact with a spirit. At no time during the session should anyone touch the medium, who is by now in a light or deep trance, and is communicating with his or her control, guide, angel, or spirits.

During the sitting, the participants should be relaxed and holding to the expectancy and belief that this will be a worthwhile sitting; keeping a sense of humor doesn't hurt either—it adds good vibrations to any session. They should try and try again if it appears to be a "slow night." The medium, it must be remembered, cannot simply turn on contact or their abilities like a light switch.

When the sitting is concluded, discussion among the participants is encouraged over what transpired. Follow-up sittings or private readings might be needed for further clarification. All members of a sitting should always remember to mentally or verbally thank the spirits for the session.

If the conditions are right and the vibrations are perfect for reception, the readings can be exceptional. It might be possible to see "balls of light" (spirit lights), or diffused shimmering light. The medium's voice could be that of somebody you once knew, a person now in spirit. It's even possible to see shadowed forms, feel cool or warm drafts, perhaps smell a familiar scent or fragrance, flowers, or an odor that was once associated with the departed.

The séance can, under the right circumstances, be a fascinating and rather exciting experience. Remember that sittings, dreams, and spirit visits, as well as Near Death Experiences, give us proof that earth death is not the end of our existence.

Benefits of the Séance

In summary, the good old-fashioned séance, either in a group or a one-on-one situation, has some very positive points to consider:

- Like-minded people can meet.

- It provides a joint process of unlocking doors to the otherside.

- A limited number of people allows for better focus.

- The environment and activity are comfortable and unhurried.

- The ritual holds people steady.

- It allows time to relax and reflect.

- Personal insight is enhanced.

- Enough time is allowed to target specific spirits, perhaps in depth.

- Important energy is exchanged in circles.

- It is an educational device to prove there is life after death.

- It is personalized.

- Relief and comfort are offered to sufferers.

- Fear of death is lessened.

- Communication with the departed is achieved.

Controversy: The Case Against Mediumship

Skeptics generally believe that apparitions are hallucinations produced by emotional needs, and that the séance is another attempt at explaining what is impossible to discover. They subscribe to any of the following ideas.

- Spirit controls and guides come from the subconscious mind of the medium.

- Messages originate from a medium with Extra Sensory Perception (ESP) who is able to intercept telepathic thoughts from clients and sitters.

- The medium has advanced background information on sitters prior to the séance.

- Spirit messages appear to be vague, garbled, and confused.

- It is sheer fraud, nonsense, and a bitter hoax.

- The client or sitter wants to believe and overlooks inconsistencies of message.

- It's not possible to make contact since the entire process is an invalid assumption.

- ESP and telepathy are obtained from a fertile imagination in many cases.

- People want to believe they see and hear apparitions.

- Dreams seem to give life to these spontaneous phenomena.

- The whole matter is rife with coincidences and reasonable explanations.

- Some of the participants need or are undergoing therapy.

- Participants suffer from intense cravings for comfort; confusion about what was observed, heard, or felt; and guilt over the deceased.

- Participants desire to attract attention.

Without being overly critical, skeptics build the barriers that cut us off from spirit contact that would allow us to find out what the scheme of our life is and what purpose it has. From spirit contact we do learn what the next life will be like, and how we should conduct our lives while living in this earth plane. Spirit contact provides us with much information, especially if we remain open and accepting. In a nutshell, there are many paths to spiritual enlightenment, and for many the acceptance of what is handed down and blessed with a traditional scientific rationale does not seem to be the total answer. Moreover, American culture must learn how to deal with its fear of death; science and medicine seem to be avoiding this can of worms.

The Ethical Medium

Because of pervasive skeptical perceptions, the medium must strive to be seen as a caring and honest individual and to that end must develop a personal code of ethical behavior that he or she can use as a guide to mediumship. Below is an initial list of items that can be deleted, added to, built upon, or used for personal introspection.

- Mediums should acknowledge their partnership with the otherside.

- Fraud, sleight of hand, tricks, exaggeration, and bluster must always be avoided.

- A medium, if paid for readings and other related events, will share a portion with charities or their church; this casts the money out to the universe and helps others. The amount of money received and given will be decided by the medium.

- Mediums will respect others' viewpoints, ideas, and diversity; they will never judge.

- True mediums recognize that they are not infallible.

- A medium will not become beholden to money or involved in politics and negative societal trends.

- A medium will not divulge private readings to others.

- A medium will educate others and make it known that death is not the ending.

- Mediums will celebrate life and their spirituality by holding joy in their hearts and will, by actions and deeds, show others that a well-lived life benefits all.

The obsession with hauntings, ghosts, and supernatural events is the "life blood" to those involved with the paranormal—it is inescapable. To the medium, dealings with the spirit world are the bread and butter of the profession. Ghost hunters have become exceedingly technical, well organized, and involved with many facets of the paranormal, which is of keen interest to most mediums and psychics.

As long as the medium follows the ethical constructs of his or her craft, adhering to the guide posts of spirituality (without question), it is a good bet that morality and ethics will serve the medium well in assisting others.

The Misuse of Abilities

It's never a good thing to do bad things in anger, especially when you discover and are able to use your abilities. I will parade two things I did out of anger when I realized I could throw my fists around. It's my negative karma accrual, and much later I received my punishments, which I won't reveal here. I do know, however, that what goes around comes around, and I got such a smack!

Coincidence?

A certain college professor and I did not see eye to eye. I felt that he had it in for me, particularly singling me out in a senior seminar class by holding my papers up for ridicule. I thought, "okay, you deserve this," and I unleashed my mind's focus on him in a daily barrage of negative vibrations. His tenure was denied, and he was let go. Oh, did I pay for this one!

Not Good!

I ran afoul—I sincerely believe I was an innocent party—of two very unpleasant supervisors at work. In my fury I concentrated my mind's power into making them sick, and sick they became. It was weeks of recovery for one, months for the other. When I fully understood what I had done, I bombarded them daily with love and healing, frantically trying to repair the damage done to them and to my eternal soul. Yes, they recovered, but my guilt lingers to this day. I did receive bad news over what I had done.

The reason this misuse of powers is noted is to warn you that you must never abuse these special abilities—there are consequences. As a further admonishment, be very careful in your Readings; never reveal the dramatic or hurtful. Everyone seems to want an aura reading, but be careful with what you tell. The same goes for dream readings and interpretations, especially if you are sure it could cause problems or sow the seeds of despair.

Cobra in a Sack

The dark side of the human personality that we all have must be contained and neutralized—it's hard at times. Try visualizing a small, venomous cobra snake in a gunnysack you are holding in your right hand, knowing that it will eventually get out of the sack, striking you and others with its deadly fangs and filling everyone with its poison. As your physical or emotional anger grows, so does the size of the cobra. It becomes heavier and heavier, larger and larger, thrashing mightily to get out and strike.

You hold the sack tightly, realizing you are giving life to your creation. You take hold of your emotions while asking your inner guide for strength and resolution to overcome this moment of spite. You visualize a mist of cool and nourishing White Light surrounding you with love and protection. With your positive and loving thoughts, the cobra sack disappears. Try this when you feel your anger and other negative emotions rising, waiting to be unleashed like that cobra.

Remember that the refinement of the art of mediumship-clairvoyance comes with a price, and it's a personal choice whether to become public or to stay in the mainstream of society. Living a day filled with minor or private miracles, or just simply enjoying a life filled with exciting things and events, can still allow a partnership in the paranormal; you are very able to keep your feet and mind on a steady path of enlightenment that benefits others and well as yourself.

The Careful Medium

In addition to practicing their craft in an ethical manner, mediums must be careful in the use of their gifts. Sometimes revealing all is not the best practice. There are four things that thwart my being completely free with my mediumistic gifts. One is mind reading. When I meet people and am readily available to read their minds, I sometimes become disturbed over what they are thinking—about "things"—and even what they think or want from me. So I immediately establish a block, feeling that I've intruded on personal ground! It can be a very scary proposition to see and feel things that should never meet the light. But as a rule, this gift has served me well in understanding people.

The second thing is aura reading. This can also be very personal, especially if the person is having a bad day, or perhaps is in ill health; you strain at telling, however you must learn to bridle your mouth. I tell the positives that I see in the aura, and the full slate of things only if I know them well or suspect that they can handle the details. Aura reading can be very revealing. It used to save my tail in a previous job I once held, and I used to couple aura reading with a little mind reading, or ESP if you will. It helped with promotions and avoiding unpleasant matters.

The third thing is avoiding unpleasant things I see in a séance session. If the person can handle it, I tell; if not, I don't. If I'm in a deep, trancelike state, it's beyond my control. And furthermore, it's delightful to meet, hug, or be kissed by spirits and your guides, and sometimes theirs!

The fourth thing to take control of and only partially share are premonitions. Avoiding unpleasant things in what you see and the events that will/could happen is always best for sparing a person's ego. It might even change that person's destiny. People become scared of you for what you reveal, and avoid you if you tell too much truth. Premonitions, or intuitive insights, can also floor you, and make you very upset. I'll give you two examples of delayed premonitions, those intuitive shocks that flash through your mind but aren't received immediately.

Princess Diana

In 1997, I was dining with my wife and a friend at one of the hot spots in town. I was happy to be in a place that had received such glowing reviews. The dining went well until I started to hear buzzing sounds and faint voices. I suddenly became agitated and depressed, and the dinner was ruined for me. I could sense something bad was happening. As we were driving home my ugly mood continued. When we reached home I turned on the television set, sitting down to calm my nerves, and there it was, Princess Diana had been killed in an automobile accident in Paris. Well, having a special affinity for her, I became distraught. This was an ugly premonition indeed!

September 11, 2001

The second premonition was also an ugly one. My wife and I were in the Boston (Logan) airport, waiting to take off to Chicago. We had been upgraded to first class, and I was eagerly waiting for breakfast (not too bad on that airline). We waited and waited for take-off, and that certain feeling came to me—problem. The buzzing in my ears and headache commenced. Eventually, the captain announced that we were to quickly disembark, and I blurted out, "Terrorists!" Several passengers and two flight attendants looked at me oddly. One of the pilots had tears streaming down his face; then I knew something was very wrong. Chaos reigned in the airport, and a few minutes later we learned why—the World Trade Towers and two other places had been struck by airplanes. Our flight was almost at the same time, and from the Boston airport; I often wonder if I would've been warned in advance by my guardians if I had been scheduled for one of the ill-fated flights.

Premonitions? Yes, I strongly believe in them, but not to the point that they govern my life. Things will and do unfold the way they were meant to happen. Can we take control over them and change their direction? I'll leave that up to you.

The Methodical Medium

It is a good idea to create an initial log for scientific validation and investigations into ghost and apparition observations as well as other séance occurrences. Here is a list of what's needed:

- Camera(s), preferably a camrecorder
- Tape recorder(s)
- Night vision goggles
- Electronic temperature devices

- No less than three scientific, theological, or dispassionate observers

And here are the procedures:

- Record time, day, and frequency of appearances or paranormal events.

- Explore and log possibilities of environmental contamination.

- Record temperatures, interior and exterior, with weather conditions.

- Log names, addresses, and occupations of participants.

- Map out area, recording exact spot of observance or feeling.

- Attempt to communicate with, or touch apparition if possible.

- Note if apparition is passive, active, aggressive, or dangerous.

- Record if they are solid, wispy, or shadowlike, and if there are odors, voices, colors, or energy emanating from apparition.

- Note the participants' thoughts and feelings.

- If this event occurs at a séance, interview medium and participants, obtaining written permission and affidavits.

- Repeat process on a following day or night if possible.

The modern day medium is up against a wall in offering concrete proof to the scientific and skeptical observer, and the previous remarks on ghost (apparition) logs can furnish proof or information to make some sort of baseline judgment.

Do I believe in ghosts? No, but I'm afraid of them.
—THE MARQUISE DU DEFFAND

Ghosts

Perhaps the reason why most people don't see or hear the spirits of the departed is because they don't expect to see, meet, or hear them. At our passing we all become beings of light or concentrated energy forms or fields. Ghosts are earth-bound spirits who can't or won't leave our earth plane, and many continue to suffer. It might be legitimately asked why ghosts want to contact us in the first place. There are many possible answers. Perhaps they:

- are scared, shocked, and confused over their new existence

- vengeful, angry, mean, and petty

- don't know what to do

- never believed in an afterlife, no options of direction

- have unfinished business on earth plane

- are afraid of being judged, want last word

- want to hang around and observe

- are unsure that loved ones are taken care of

- are afraid of what they'll find out

- don't want to meet others in an afterlife they didn't get along with while living

- are curious

- refuse to accept the status of their death

- prefer their last living environment to the unknown.

Another thing to consider is that since like attracts like, some of us act as magnets of attraction to earth-bound spirits, and our fear feeds them; they draw on our energy or vibrational force.

Clarification is needed for the scientific community, in particular parapsychologists, when it comes to spirits, hauntings, and methodology. Unless it is for "soul rescue" purposes—cleansing a place from haunting by making contact and informing the spirit (ghost) that they are dead or not wanted—the medium does not make a deliberate attempt to contact earth-bound entities, because there is a chance of running into malevolent or lower spirit forms. In some instances spirits slip through and refuse to leave. There can be a lot of emotional pain, loneliness, fear, and angst in the reluctant spirit that has to be dealt with. The medium or psychic must be able to size up these spirit emotions and approach the rescue with empathy or a heavy hand.

Usually, however, the medium is focused primarily on contacting the higher spirit forms beyond the earth plane. In the next chapter, "Into the Invisible Realm," this will be discussed, and as for mediums being susceptible to ESP and mental telepathy, as in all things, we will believe what we want to believe.

The Advanced Medium

The medium's challenge is to "see." There is a price to be exacted for the ability to be a medium or clairvoyant, whether active or inactive. One can choose to do limited readings for friends, family, and a selected clientele, or one can be willing to pay a high price in energy and psychic depletion to become a local or nationally known personality.

Many choose to live a life in the shadows, which allows a somewhat "normal" life of marriage, healthy relationships, employment, car and mortgage payments, raising children, and generally participating in life's mainstream, unnoticed and not tagged as being "weird" or strange and treated as somehow "different."

It is exciting to be able to use a plethora of precognitive abilities and be able to second-guess society's trends, to be forewarned and forearmed, if you will. Self-awareness, enlightenment, and self-actualization, if done on a path that helps others as well as yourself, can lead a person to live life as a secret hero. It is all well and good to have faith and belief in the esoteric arts, but action is required or the entire process is hollow; wishing doesn't make it so. It is the choice of declared medium-clairvoyants to be out front, refraining from wrapping themselves in a cloak of mysticism, or to choose to dabble here and there, while still remaining a personality that society can accept and identify with as a "regular" person.

The advanced medium will be able to extract readings by way of séances, psychometry, scrying from crystal balls or water, or by using candles. Mediumship is not witchcraft; it is holding expectancy, and interpreting events by seeing via meditation, prayer, dreams, listening to that certain feeling, and being open to the environment.

A relaxed body and mind obtained from sufficient sleep, recreational outlets, exercise, and proper nourishment, mixed with doses of good emotional health and a generous foundation of faith and belief, all set into motion by action and practice, possibly leads to and through the door of the invisible world.

It takes much more than reading several books and attending a few seminars to find what's out there and then simply delving into the principals and practice of the paranormal arts. An interested party must meet those working in the area. There is no substitute for a study circle or socializing with a like-minded group for testing the waters.

Enhancements on the path of discovery and unlocking those abilities can be found through great amounts of meditation, Reiki healing, yoga breathing methods and exercise, Zen meditation and philosophy, tai chi exercise, and tarot card reading and interpretation; the list seems to be endless. It's much easier said than done, right? Well, it's up to the individual to go beyond interest and beginning mediumship in order to reach an advanced state of expertise.

Hollywood delights its audience by furnishing exciting paranormal dramas, but in reality the real thing doesn't happen in a two-hour movie or a television series; interesting and fun, yes, but reality takes far more time to be revealed.

The ultimate goal of life beyond Hollywood scenarios is to live and learn the best we can and to share real happiness with others. Love for others, as well as self, frees the heart from earthly bonds and lets us fly. The same can be said of kindness. Practice love and forgiveness— drop the negatives that can blind you to who you are.

Surely esoteric and paranormal secrets will result in a well-balanced state of inner harmony that makes all of us liberated and free souls. Mediumship holds some of these answers.

Helping Others to Manifest Their Wishes

The following simple exercise will help others as well as yourself to manifest desires and wishes, and will lead to personal insight. I was taught this method many years ago by my mentor before it became a regular trick of the trade in self-discovery conferences. Any medium can assist others by this method, and it can be considered a special gift from the universe.

1. Focus your mind on what you want (goals, desires, wishes); know what you want; be sure you really want it. A meditative state is the best way to focus.

2. Imprint your desires in your subconscious mind by writing them down or by drawing pictures; verbalize your wish out loud; this will send it out to the universe. Only one wish at a time, or it will confuse the issue.

3. Imagine that you have or will realize this wish or goal soon. Visualize what it will be like to obtain this desire—go into details. Visualize your thoughts going out to the universe several times.

4. Follow your intuition by looking for the signs that something is happening.

5. Know for sure that this is really what you want—be confident.

6. Repeat and repeat these steps without becoming obsessive.

7. Feel, believe, and know that the universe will help you.

8. Attempt to follow up this desire with action on your part—if possible, give it a push.

Always remember that we construct our own reality; the universe and ourselves are one. With this exercise, we open our minds to the infinite that all things are possible. Call on your spirit guides for help.

We can certainly see from this extensive chapter of lists that mediumship is an art or craft that has been with us for many years, perhaps thousands of years, in several world cultures and civilizations. To blow off mediumship's survival through the ages as mankind's defaulting to superstition in a historically unsettled world does not answer the question. Why does it continue to survive in the light of scientific rationale and inquiry? With all of the tremendous advances being made in our ultra-technological-materialistic world, why does the medium's craft and it's involvement with death continue to hold interest—and participants? Some call it the sin of necromancy—worshipping and talking to the dead—but as we know, every sin has its own avenging angel.

Into the Invisible Realm 4

Only logical reasoning and pure mathematics seem to be above aggressive skepticism. Granted, scientific theory can arrive at strong probabilities, but no absolute is feasible in this universe of ours. Probability is still speculation. When we come to the issue of death and the subsequent survival of personality after or during that death, we are again met with conjecture. The theory that death will reduce the physical body to a state of corruption and dust, literally speaking, is a fairly good assumption.

Then we come to the scientific assumption concerning the brain-mind-thoughts equation, which according to science and medicine also dies with the body; we arrive at a point of speculative probability, maybe even at an absolute declaration that the personality does not survive the transition from the physical state of death to nothingness.

When it is stated that there are no real absolutes in our lives, our planet, or in our universe we come closer to probability. It takes a leap of faith to believe that something or somebody created the universe and all living creatures, no matter what form they've taken. A further leap of faith is required to believe that the sum total of the human personality survives beyond physical death. Then a further gigantic leap of faith is required to believe that there is an afterlife and another place of residence to receive the departed soul.

Many individuals, including this author, who temporarily died and took this fabulous journey to the otherside, feel their lives were touched and forever changed. They went through that tunnel, into the famous light, where they caught glimpses of what the next life could bring. It becomes rather difficult to debate the skeptic's negative response because it is hard to furnish concrete proof of that visit. However, these people know what occurred during their very personal Near Death Experience. Medical and scientific investigators say such experiences happen because:

- the individual is under anesthesia or sedation;

- drug intoxication or medication reaction occurs;

- there is cerebral anoxia and a lack of oxygen to the brain;

- stress endorphins are released in heavy doses;

- the individual is reliving the birth canal experience;

- temporal lobe paroxysm problems occur; the brain short-circuits

- of severe trauma, hallucinations are produced.

And the question is this: If there's so much smoke, where is the fire? Intense NDEs do happen. Many reasons concerning these experiences can be offered, but instead of using the scientific rationale as an easy brush-off and shield, further investigations are needed.

The Invisible Realm

Is it a true statement that if God didn't exist, then humans would have to invent such a being? That if an afterlife didn't exist, or if the soul didn't exist, then humans would have to develop some fabrication for continuance and comfort?

Mediums, Spiritualists, Theosophists, some religions, and others that deal with paranormal phenomena have long believed that another dimension as yet unknown to science, or a parallel universe, is the other world of the spirit realm. This invisible world, divulged through many years of spirit communications, can be simplified and divided into several levels or astral planes:

LEVEL I: the earth plane, which is next to and merges with our existence. This is the plane where the spirit's journey commences, where the spirit's (soul) energy force commences its first step on its journey. It is also the level from which those who have died will not, or cannot, leave. Their transition is held back by confusion, love of the material existence they left behind, guilt, and fear. For those who are weighed down with terrible deeds committed while alive, this plane could be construed as their personal hell, their self-created reality.

LEVEL II: possibly the second step in the journey—the tunnel and the light. It is the receiving room where the life review and orientation process for Level III attainment takes place, also where the soul/spirit is met by guide or angel.

LEVEL III: beyond the first two levels. This is Summerland, paradise, or heaven. This level is where the perfection and education of the soul/spirit is commenced, the beginning of the transfiguration into the energy force and matter of the universe. Reincarnation is said to take place at this level if willed.

LEVEL IV: and beyond, merging with the universe is completed—a "Nirvana," a total heaven and unity with the universe; an eternity or infinite amount of "time."

An Alternate View of the Astral Planes, or Levels of Eternity

Plane VIII: Pure and complete oneness with the universe—"Nirvana"—"One with the Universe"

Plane VII: Total and final assimilation in the universe

Plane VI: Understanding of all Cosmic Knowledge (Mental)

Plane V: Where all of mankind synthesizes Wisdom (Mental)

Plane IV: Knowledge, training, preparation for eternal evaluation, the last plane of human and earth familiarity—"Summerland"—Heaven—Paradise

Plane III: Orientation and "shake-down" plane; adjustments to deceased condition commences—Transition—The Awakening

Plane II: The "payoff" plane for evil and the dissolute—place of hauntings and the tragedies of human character (Pandora's Box)—Purgatory—Hell—Nothingness—Suspension

Plane I: Physical reality—Earth

Planes I and II almost merge. Mediums have best contact with Planes II, III, and IV.

Cosmic Optimism—the Afterlife

Pythagoras surmised that "the human soul is immortal, for it resembles the heavenly stars, and like them is involved in perpetual motion and shining in its brightness." Expanding loosely on this thought, the proof of survival would most assuredly come from a laundry list of phenomena observed:

- apparitions of the dead (hundreds of thousands of cases noted)
- deathbed observations, comments, and visions
- spirit visits
- Electronic Voice Phenomena (EVP), i.e., radios, tape-recorders, computers, etc.
- poltergeists
- possessions by a spirit force
- mediums and their information
- NDEs and OBEs
- reincarnation
- telepathic voices and messages
- miracles
- various other assorted psychic phenomena

As a layman, it is difficult to offer concrete proof on the existence of an afterlife and the survival of the human ego and personality unless you've had intimate experiences or made the short journey via an NDE or an OBE. If you've had an experience, there are few people you would trust with the information, because it's only natural to avoid being labeled strange and not the sharpest knife in the drawer.

On the other hand, some of us are believers but we don't know why—actually we want desperately to believe that we continue after death, but we know enough to exercise caution over being swept-away in gullibility and vulnerability. Following are some questions that many have on the subject of the afterlife, and the responses that I would give to them.

Where and how do all of the spirit energy forces fit into these planes—thinking of all the people who have ever lived and who will ever live?

The universe is infinite, so there is infinite room/space for all that have lived or will ever live. Remember that matter/mass can fit any space.

Can we go back and forth between these levels, or planes?

If we have the strength of force and the desire to—also think of reincarnation, but it is supposed that transmigration can only occur between Levels II and III, because the higher levels are where the merger with the total universe commences.

What is the purpose of levels (astral planes)?

Think of these levels as a structure imposed as a grand design by the universe, in which it is too vast to comprehend and beyond understanding.

How do we know what we think we know about these astral planes or levels?

Our root understanding comes from many thousands of spirit communications, spirit visits, mediums, "holy" people, readings, and by visits through OBEs and NDEs.

What goes on in these levels?

Orientation, lessons, education, and assimilation of the knowledge of our planet and of the universe, keeping in mind that it is a new and eternal life completely separate from this one.

Will we ever meet the individuals and loved ones who have been instrumental in our life's journey?

Very possible, especially if they are/were spiritual souls involved with you and if they chose to be in this Summerland, and their spirituality is "clean." Love and strong bonds seems to be a magnet there as it was here.

Why are these astral planes kept separate from us while we are living?

There are two different worlds for a purpose. Earth is our first schoolhouse (no matter how many reincarnations, if undertaken); the afterlife is our second. Earth's humanity with its many institutions and various societies would collapse with total revelation. We would not be able to work out the personal drama of good versus evil, thereby losing the force of our free will—our basic education on this earth plane. Avoidance of striving for personal spirituality during difficult times would not let us know what we are made of. We must all go through these vital testing periods. Whether we accrue good karma or bad karma, our life's lessons and deeds shape the emphasis of our positioning in the next life, likened to the beginner, intermediate, or advanced student.

Will we be able to do "earth" things over there?

To certain degrees at first. Our earthly endeavors, such as sports, sex, eating, and so on, are part of the gentle transition or orientation process. These earth-important needs seem to be quickly discarded as meaningless when new options are added like education, knowledge, music, healing, and communication with the living, all leading to learning and acting as spirit guides and angels, while entering the phase of this new "life."

What will I look like?

In the adaptation of acquiring new roles, you can be fifteen or eighty years old, and whatever physical condition you deem important to your disappearing ego, you can discard all diseases and infirmities if desired. Everything is based on thoughts. You can move by thought, think by thought, and communicate by thought. Eventually, depending on your needs and ability, you shed the illusion of the earth form and materialize to spirit, which is a small mass of colored energy, or "globes."

What does this new world look like?

It depends on what your thoughts want it to be: forests, mountains, plains, seashore, grand houses, flower gardens, slums, a lone cabin in a snow field, cities or a town. The endless possibilities of beauty are beyond our comprehension and are basically dependent on what your mind wants. There is only wonder, perfection, and goodness in this Summerland, or heaven. With the cessation of earthly mind clutter, periods of great mind bending and originality occur—there are no longer any limitations.

What are the steps, if any, for entering into this new "life?"

1. Complete physical death.

2. Entering into a period of confusion and disorientation, which usually lasts as long as ten earth days (or more); a spirit guide or angel (usually your guardian angel) will escort you to the Plane of Adjustment (Level II), where you will undergo a Life Review process, a rerun of your life comprised of every second you've ever lived.

3. The decision to transmigrate to Summerland, or heaven, depends on the amount of spiritual, negative, or positive baggage you are carrying (by the universe?), and on how long the process will take—a sorting out period. Those who were so heavily involved with the material world (earth) or had a surplus of bad deeds stay in the never world of transition for earth generations, and possibly end up as lower forms—ghosts, malevolent spirits, or such. These entities are earth-bound in Level I. This could be considered a "Hell on earth."

4. The first real transmigration, Level III, is beyond the other two levels. This is the plane where perfection of the soul is worked on, and the beginning of the transmigration into the universe. The orientation and adjustment phase, as mentioned previously, occurs in Summerland. This is the last plane of human and earth familiarity.

5. The rest of the Levels, or astral planes, the ones for merging into the universe, take an infinity of preparation.

NOTE: Time frames of transitional phases vary with each soul or energy force, taking into account that there are no time considerations in the universe.

For another view of the death orientation process, spiritual baggage, what negative and positive deeds can do to you or for you, souls and guides, read *The Divine Comedy: Purgatorio,* by Dante Alighieri, written in Italy in the 1200s. It comes in a lengthy poem or prose format and is heavily metaphysical, insightful, and church-driven propaganda, weaving spiritual beliefs, actions, and numerous truths into what we perhaps can anticipate in the next dimension.

A Case of Spiritual Connection

During a vacation in southern England with wife and friends, I became overwhelmed with a flood of emotions, intense feelings, and vibrations whenever we went into a graveyard, cathedral, or church. Keenly interested in touching monuments and headstones in an attempt to attract or discern vibrations from every historical building, monument, and tombstone, I became profoundly disoriented because of the tingling sensations that I received.

I was spiritually confused while touring Stonehenge, that fantastic monument sitting on the Salisbury Plain, built by early man's raw strength and religious zeal for the purpose of understanding the universe, with gigantic stones for celestial information, probably for the purpose of plotting religious holidays and the planting and harvesting of crops. I could feel the vibrations emanating from the stone pillars and the ground they stood on. There was a protective fence around the stones and we were unable to get as close as we wanted, but I could still feel the pull of vibrations. I sincerely believed that I heard the sounds of voices and chanting through a cold and blustery day.

Later, we spent time in the awe-inspiring Salisbury cathedral, and with sarcophagi, crypts, and earthly remains of noted individuals buried beneath the cathedral floor, the intense vibrations continued. With further visits to Winchester cathedral, the graves of Sir Arthur Conan Doyle, T. E. Lawrence (Lawrence of Arabia), the Churchill family, and several very old Anglo-Saxon churches and their graveyards, the vibrations were intense enough for me to experience continuous tingles in my hands, feet, and head.

We stayed at a converted nunnery and monastery built in 1066, now a magnificent hotel, haunted by a nun who just happened to take ghostly residence in the suite of rooms my wife and I were staying in. The tragic story of her life and terrible demise increased the intensity of the vibrations in the suite of rooms, and being somewhat inured to spirits, I could still feel her presence and slept with the light on—as if that could do anything.

As a medium, why was I bothered over these vibrations and a supposed ghost? Because, I've always felt like an intruder in the invisible world. What would I do, could I do, after I made spirit contact outside of a protective séance circle or spirit communication session, with friends and a wife who would stare at my strange behavior? What would happen if an accidental or premeditated contact with a powerful lower form was committed, and with nonbelieving witnesses?

In Spirit Rescue, a committed group of psychics or clairvoyants attempt to release confused, bewildered, and scared spirits, but at least we have an idea—perhaps, of who they once were and what they wanted. For a medium, a séance, a reading, or a soul rescue is a draining, exhausting proposition that must be undertaken in optimum and positive conditions, and when away from a protective environment, what can be done while encountering spirits on their turf?

In a haunted house I once lived in, the conditions should have been optimum in my control of events. One half of the house was mine and the other half was theirs. Sounds fair? This particular spirit would present itself on Wednesday evenings around 9:00. The smell of burning feathers or hair—the odor varied—was an announcement of presence, accompanied with a cool draft. I burned candles and said the soul rescue oath of release. It would help momentarily, but the spirit visit would occur again in the days or weeks ahead.

Oh yes, I checked the house for electrical problems, and odors were also checked outside the house, in case the neighbors were using their fireplaces (in the summer?). A spirit cleansing was attempted by a friend, which seemed to help for a short period of time. I won't go into my mother-in-law's sightings of a being with red eyes, which might have been one of the principal causes for her moving out (didn't want to discuss it), and all the other things that happened, such as clothes being moved in closets, loud footsteps and noises, and so on. These events happened with no harm being done to anyone. The vibrations in the house remained positive despite a cluster of unusual happenings.

We found out later that two tragedies had occurred in the history of the house, and we later moved, not from fear, but because we no longer needed a large house. I suspect several families have since played host to these spiritual residents, and provided they are receptive and sensitive to these beings, they could have had some interesting experiences.

These experiences were reflected upon for the main purpose of indicating that spirit encounters—with major and minor events—can occur in daily life, especially if one is receptive and alert. A few individuals among us, perhaps you are one, can feel vibrations from old houses, monuments, battlefields, and objects—actually it can be fun and rather interesting, it's all in connecting with the environment. A person does not have to dally in the occult as a sorcerer, seer, or soothsayer to be aware of what happened, what is happening, or what will happen. Many people who deal in the supernatural believe that paranormal events occur around us on a daily basis, especially through dreams. Over all, vibrations from many seemingly mundane occurrences and spirit visits are frequently ignored, or when observed physically, are set aside as coincidences or a rampant imagination at work.

Paths into the Invisible Realm

In addition to the séance techniques described in the previous chapter there are a number of other ways of connecting with the invisible realm.

Electronic Voice Communication

You might try the electronic method of spirit communication. Place a tape recorder in a quiet room or when everyone has gone to bed. Put in an hour-long tape initially. The next day, play it back for noise, especially static, you might even hear strange noises or voices. If you don't have success at first, keep trying; the sounds can be rather interesting.

Psychometry

By touching or holding objects, you can pick up vibrations and mental pictures of the owner and "see" or feel a person's vibrations, an event, or perhaps something that has happened or will happen. This method of visioning is called psychometry. Other sensitives and psychics like to touch tombstones, monuments, and objects in order to pick up mental pictures.

This I did in England and at an old graveyard in Portsmouth, New Hampshire, for the express purpose of attempting to see into other dimensions. It has been a useful exercise for assisting friends over the years, and it was used in a spiritual unfoldment class I once took to assist a local police department in the solving of a few crimes. Psychometry is an art derived from meditation and concentration; it's a great parlor trick if it doesn't hurt anyone—always ask permission!

Energy Scars

It is believed by many students of the occult that past or present personalities and events leave an imprint on a room, house, business, field of battle, or wherever a meeting or conflict occurred, leaving behind "energy scars" or "residue hauntings." It's also possible to feel spirit energy when they come back to the place where they were at the time of their death or where they once were happiest and most secure.

This short blurb is to indicate the mind's ability at picking up messages and visions if a person is truly interested in spirit contact or looking into events, past and present. The key question here: Is it an illusion? Like clairvoyance, death, and the invisible world, we question what this is all really about.

Prophecy

Now, a few words about prophecy, the art of seeing into the past and the future. Other words and terms for this visioning are oracles, seers, soothsayers, wizards, "the sight," navi, divination, inspired vision, revelation, prophets, and witchcraft. There are many famous people throughout time gifted as prophets who had the ability to forecast future events—Jesus, Muhammad, the Buddha, Moses, Nostradamus, and Edgar Cayce seem to stand out in instant recall; however, there were many other prophets in various religions, now and yesterday; the Biblical prophets certainly can not be overlooked.

Prophecy is accomplished by clearing the mind while in a deep meditative state, deep enough that the entire environment almost seems to disappear. A practiced individual can make good use of aides such as the tarot, scrying, the crystal ball, astrology, and most certainly dreams. The advanced medium must be adept in forecasting things to come.

Personal Revelations

For this book, as well as with my previous one, I spent several hours a day for weeks looking into the future (by candles, meditation, and scrying). I saw the future events listed below, always taking into account that the universe and spirit helpers on the otherside were not time constrained as I was. I have not revealed everything in depth or even everything I saw, because I dislike being an alarmist; but, here it is.

- Death and dying centers will become the worldwide norm (or commence) roughly by 2030; I believe because of short falls in medicine—and its expense—overpopulation, shortfalls in food and good water, and an ugly existence.

- There will be an official U.S. government devaluation of currency—fifty cents to a dollar. This will be because of fierce competition in trade with the unified trading blocks of Asia, Europe, and South America in about 2012. This measure will not help our exporting sales.

- Organized religion as we now understand it, in America and Europe, will fragment and quasi-Christian cults and sects will become the next "religions." This will be a gradual evolution and will be somewhat noticeable by 2018 and after; this will be a peaceful movement. The religion of Islam will cease to dominate their societies due to shortages of food and water, and harsh dictatorships. They will war with their neighbors for arable land.

- AIDS will remain out of control, propelled by new strains, resulting in a horrendous number of deaths in the world; now, and to the end of this century.

- There will be phenomenal breakthroughs in medicine for presently untreatable diseases, coming with a very high price tag; couldn't see the diseases to be helped by these new medications; there will be many types of new medicines by 2014 because of a "central discovery."

- America and Europe will be overwhelmed by mass immigration and fertile populations from third world countries, putting an enormous strain on existing resources such as food, building materials, land, and water. Intense demand for the few manufactured goods available, and infrastructures—physical and social—will take place by 2030 or 2040.

- There will be a breakthrough in spirit contact and communication by electronic means about 2020. This breakthrough has the potential of upsetting our cultural and societal structure.

- An increase of spirituality (the new religion) will spread across the world, because of a hope for a better life. There will be a new spiritual teacher and leader (a tall, dark-headed, light-skinned, green-eyed, married male in his late twenties), from southeastern India, who will spread hope, love, and a "different" kind of eternity. I don't see him as a charlatan; his earthly birth occurs in November of 2010.

- The institution of "temporary marriage" on a trial basis, with renewals being every five years, will become officially sanctioned in the United States and Canada around 2016; children resulting from these marriages will become wards of the state if the marriage is not renewed.

- In the United States, college entrance will be based on a strict lottery system, money, status, and very high test scores, because of limited resources and classroom space, by mid century. It also seems that most applicants in this lottery system will be female because the majority of males will seem to see little value in a college education, preferring apprenticeship and trade schools.

- The United States will hold together only because of tradition; the Northeast, South, Southwest, Upper Midwest, and

West Coast will become the geographic and social divisions; Hawaii, Alaska, and Puerto Rico will be separate entities entirely. This weak confederation will come about because of ethnic populations, economics, and diverse politics and cultural directions. These divisions are actually occurring now and will be more apparent by 2050.

- Populations across the world will surrender most of their rights and liberties for military safety and economic security; in effect now, accomplishment by 2070 in many countries.

- Numerous miniwars will flare up across the world around 2025—over drugs, religion, population shifts, border containment, and economics.

- Much of the earth's green vegetation will permanently turn to faded yellow shades because of the holes in the ozone layer, stripping chlorophyll from all forms of vegetation— really apparent by 2030. The oceans in many places of the world will virtually turn into moving cesspools because of excessive dumping. Note: several scenarios were seen on the environment and its effect on human habitation, customs, and societies—none very good—and most, sadly, are now irreversible.

- No time frame: Israel will become a more thriving and vibrant country despite occasional outbreaks of terrorism. A very interesting thing was seen while scrying. It seems that this country and its people "of faith," "will continue to be protected" by the spirits and angels of past Roman, European, and Nazi persecution. This was an amazing, interactive vision.

Entering the Invisible Realm

When we attempt the transition from life to death, entering into the astral levels, we can undergo a dangerous and vulnerable condition called spirit (soul) stress, in which we can feel:

- disconnected

- self-destructive (I don't want to go there)

- a lack of enthusiasm

- argumentative

- low empathy to condition

- drained of energy

- callous to condition

- disbelief

- apathy

- anger and hostility

If we're still not letting go of who we once were, of the material goods we had or didn't have, and are still clinging tightly to hates, lusts, anger and anxieties, needs and desires, then an incredible amount of energy is lost, and the release becomes terribly difficult. Spirit stress then takes over and the soul may become earth-bound. I repeat: the danger in passage to the invisible world is in being overly attached to the earth plane.

These problems, however, do not occur for spiritual individuals who do not have so strong an attachment to the earth plane. These souls will be helped by guardian angels or spirit guides. The more joy and wonderment the person feels entering the realm—almost an ecstatic state of mind—the much higher the vibrational level. We quickly learn, if we are spiritually washed and "clean," that the heaven we seek is what we make it: a center for learning, peace, a special land-scape with particular meaning to us. It's based on the energy we give it—the energy we emit is the power station that we create. This new world is like a vast canvas that we paint and that takes on a life of its own. Many know this next plane as Summerland.

Summerland

In the 1840s a twenty-four-year-old man, Andrew Jackson Davis, the "Poughkeepsie Seer" of New York State, would enter into a deep trance in which he claimed to communicate and visit with spirits in an astral plane—the "place of illusion," which he classified as the initial resting place after death. This plane was a location of bliss, rest, and harmony. It supposedly was a place with spiritual desires and pleasures minus all of the drawbacks of life, literally a paradise, or heaven, created by the mind of the deceased. The spirit's reality could create its own reality and therefore could fill a landscape with beauty, schools, cities, gardens, and homes. It was so perfect a place that is was a perpetual "Summerland" of perfection. He eventually wrote several well-received and influential books describing mediumship and this spirit world, the two most popular books being *Harmonial Philosophy* and *The Principles of Nature*. The term Summerland has been used ever since.

Generally, Davis describes the cycles the deceased go through on their journey of afterlife discovery:

- passage of the soul through a period of darkness

- movement through a tunnel

- entering an area of extremely bright light

- meeting with a spirit guide or divinelike presence

- undergoing a review of their previous life with spirit guides

- making a decision to stay earth-bound or going on to a higher plane

It does seem that Summerland, or heaven, is the transcendental plane in which the deceased meets and greets a spirit team, relatives, ancestors, friends, and lovers, a place in which the presence of higher beings and angels are in evidence. And it is extremely interesting that the concept of a Summerland-heaven continues to be gleaned from Near Death Experiences, deathbed visions, pseudo-Christian cults, and several worldwide religions.

Reincarnation

The idea of reincarnation has been with mankind for thousands of years and is the basic belief of Buddhists and Hindus. Many thousands of people in the Western world also believe in this return to the earthly plane. Past-life regressions of individuals under hypnosis, many under rigorous clinical conditions, seem to lend credence to this afterlife revolving door.

Reincarnation studies indicate that the average number of past lives is four to five rebirths, some over a span of several thousand years, and a few have many more lifetimes on record. What is so compelling about these subjects who have had past-life regressions is their ability to relate accurately languages that are obscure and dead. Moreover, the subjects also have knowledge about the time period and such mundane things as foods, customs, prices of goods, money, weather conditions, dress, and the people of their times. Usually they were not queens, kings, barons, or historical figures, but common people living placid lives, and they varied from rich to poor. The switching of genders, ages, and geography was also quite common. People such as Henry Ford, Benjamin Franklin, and General George Patton were strong believers in reincarnation, having had such experiences themselves or knowing of others who had them. Many other famous people throughout history have claimed experiences or strong beliefs in reincarnation, and most were mentally well-balanced individuals.

Another interesting point extracted from reincarnation studies is that these people relate experiences of their souls and a place like Summerland that contains spirit guides and angels. Many classify themselves as old souls, young souls, and new souls. They also feel their rebirths were highly voluntary, reentry to the earth plane being done to work off previous negative karma or to garner experiences for higher-plane development.

A fascinating facet of hypnosis in past-life regression is that patients can be rid of phobias, emotional traumas, and physical problems. This author went through several past-life regressions over a period of time, only to discover violent deaths as soldiers, priests with drinking problems, and involvement with plagues, leaving me with the question of why bother to reincarnate again if the past several lives were so negative. What possible, positive experiences can be accrued from a continuous parade of painful lives? This is obviously a question that must remain unanswered in this life, because the time to make the personal decision on reincarnation will remain over there.

Conclusions

The astral planes, or levels, are meant to be the periods of transition, mainly for the purpose of acquiring knowledge and experiences. The human personality in the form of material energy, or soul, transmigrates to further options. The afterworld, mainly a blissful, kindly, perfect paradise, such as a Summerland, should be the main staging area of choice for the deceased.

The express purpose of the afterlife is to attain rest and to accrue knowledge, but we do seem, as human beings, to have the ability of creating our own reality here and over there; our desires are taken into this equation for the next world.

- We can be any age we want, any form, if we want it—energy or past physical appearance.

- Scenery and environment is created by thought; clothing is created by thought; infirmities and disease vanish; physical movement is by thought.

- We are governed by happiness and well-being.

- Ancestors, relatives, family, lovers, and pets are present.

- Knowledge and education is a continual process; orientation and teaching is by spirits, angels, and other higher forms.

- We can see and feel things via the mind, and even touch and smell.

- Communication occurs from the mind.

- All anger, hate, lust, desires, and negative emotions are gone.

As in all things, there are problems in reaching the initial stage of bliss. If we've committed "sins" against others and ourselves or carry heavy materialistic baggage and harbor a base refusal to understand and practice spirituality, then transmigration can be thwarted or frozen. We are well aware that every sin has its avenging angel, and the avenging aspect of a disregard for personal spirituality exacts a heavy price.

The next chapter, which is on achieving and maintaining a spiritual aspect will hopefully offer an insight into a good dose of soul washing and soul repair. We all have the free will to exercise and choose options—it is one of the best gifts that the universe has offered us—along with our lives.

If a man speak or act with evil thoughts,
Pain will surely follow him,
Even as the wheel follows the ox
That drags the cart along.
—FROM THE BUDDHIST MAHA-VAGGA

Spirituality, Soulwash, and Repair 5

The soul attracts that which it secretly harbors; that which
It loves, and also that which it fears.

—JAMES ALLEN

It takes more than an eager embrace of New Age philosophy to attain spirituality, that certain state of grace, the sense of well being that we all seek. Keeping personal journals, attending "get well" seminars, joining an ashram, practicing yoga and the tai chi arts, using incense and crystals, a cursory belief in the great universal consciousness, and chanting mantras in Sanskrit do not always answer the needs that many of us pursue, knowingly or unknowingly, in our lives.

Spirituality is best defined as living, thinking, feeling, and breathing in a state of harmony and balance, with yourself, others, and the environment. Spirituality becomes, and is, a philosophy and action orientation about living life to the fullest—and with meaning.

When an individual acquires patience, humility, calmness, insight, concentration, kindness, and gentleness, then an almost complete embrace of spirituality occurs. We can even let go of the mental limitations that the self or others have imposed.

Is spirituality a tangible or material thing that we touch, feel, smell, taste, or hear? Does it really affect that undefined essence called soul? Can spirituality become ingrained as part of our being, our supernatural self? Can we employ it as a quality that leads to spiritual awakening now, and in preparation for the end of earth life and the journey beyond?

The rock-strewn path of adversity leading to the discovery and development of the spiritual self and then reaching the distant plateau of spiritual unfolding has been likened to traveling through life in darkness, without a guide or map, even a flashlight.

We must hold and be anchored in the belief that life is a beautiful thing. The old adage of, "Life is like a picture, paint it well," does have relevance. A human life journey is divided into three main chapters: birth, living, and death. Yet many of us are clueless, even with the brilliant array of paints available, about how to paint the canvas of the all-important second chapter of our lives, living.

Much of the construction in building a successful and happy life, *if* we accept spirituality as a major facet of our being, lies in not scrambling to accumulate possessions while searching for the "perfect" life. We don't have to intimidate our mate, lovers, friends, and the community with this abundance of accumulation; instead, we need to strike a harmonious balance in getting and giving back to the universe. At some point it becomes futile to make more money, to have an excess of security, of "stuff," then discover an emptiness we can't seem to fill. We eventually find ourselves living in a state of spiritual poverty. No matter how much posturing we do to impress others and ourselves, we feel more disconnected. Perhaps this is the time to construct a new spiritual house for a revamped ego.

Sigmund Freud's Keys—an Answer to Ego Problems?

A roadblock in the quest for harmony and balance in one's life journey might possibly be an ego problem. Sigmund Freud, that early pioneer of mind and emotions, propounded a model concept, an idea that all human behavior results from the interaction of three key systems.

The first system is the *id* ("it"), our innate, primitive, instinctual drive, a reservoir of our unconscious mind ruled by strong instinct, which basically means hunger, thirst, aggression, and sexuality. Destructive and aggressive urges and the "pleasure principle" are also contained in the id, demanding immediate gratification, usually without concern for moral considerations.

The second system is the *ego* ("I"), which filters or translates the id mechanism into more reasonable reactions to the environment, or in other words, survival without destroying the self or others—the "reality principle." The id leans heavily on the ego and if the base instincts of the id take control, then the force of the ego becomes the primary force or drive for action, satisfaction, and relief. Negative aggressive behavior can come out of this system.

The third system is the *superego* ("super I" or "super me"), containing the restraints of societies' learned moral values, whether they are a veneer or are deeply rooted, commonly called the "conscience"— good or bad, moral or immoral. This superego system acts as a governor on our passions and desires, strong or weak, to restrain the ego when a struggle surfaces. This one acts as the censor, and contains the values of self, family, and society.

All three systems interact and connect with each other. If one is out of balance and suppressed, restrained, weak, or too strong, then disharmony in the human organism occurs. Concern with the body, emotional yearnings, or desire for material objects can leave the self with an aggressive nature or an empty feeling. When the ego controls are lowered and weak, anxieties can occur, possibly leading to a total imbalance of the ego, and thus, problems.

Then we run across the *libido* (repressed energy), our biological and sexual drive wild card, which can rotate, rearrange, and add turmoil to the other three systems, acting as the spoiler. The libido contains such forces as anxiety, fear, guilt, shame, aggression, and loneliness.

Of course, Dr. Freud's theories are oversimplified in this explanation, must be taken as a matter of faith, and certainly are not based on hard scientific evidence, but many students in the field of the mind and emotions believe Freud hit paydirt in this basic explanation of the human psyche; other pioneers in the area of spirituality strongly believe his findings can be considered an excellent touchstone for self-discovery. The tag line to Freud's research is to be aware of the possibilities.

It is almost impossible to be a full-time "spiritual warrior," a being that has overcome ego demands, who lives in a state of grace and can at will raise a mental shield of positive energy protection from the realworld negatives of hostility, anger, stress, and anxiety, thereby avoiding being sideswiped in one's progress in the great adventure of life.

In order to live in a truly peaceful and joy-filled state, we have to contemplate these points: We are here. We were meant to be here. What is *here* really about?

If we are indeed children of the universe, what is our real purpose and what are we waiting to discover? Is our life a mere collection of random events? Do we really have free will or are our lives merely fate controlled? Is the price too high to be a spiritual person or warrior, and are we not able or willing to pay the toll? Is self-discovery and spiritual action for others, and we'll adjust later when we have the time?

Then some of us live in a state of spiritual apartheid. We practice some fragmented aspects of spirituality half-heartedly and deny the other half. Giving in to our spiritual side seems to be weighed with skepticism and confusion, as if it is a sign of personal weakness and surrender to New Age nonsense. This internal conflict, the willingness to seek out intimacy and happiness, is easier to submerge in old comfortable habits of loneliness and insecurities, thereby leaving an unbalanced ego in charge.

Could it be that the ego stands in the way of self-fulfillment? Surface appearance or surrender does not seem to equal the reality we understand or one that would fit our current self-image. Perhaps gathering material goods and status, and persisting in our certain way of doing things—our way or no way—has worked best for ego gratification, but for how long can it continue?

Releasing negative influences that hinder positive spiritual development requires preparation and revamping, a cleansing if you will. Many individuals may be unsure of how to commence a release, and they remain confused on the steps needed to rid themselves of that hollow, anxious, ego-propelled defense mechanism. Three paths can be taken.

Three Simple Paths to Spiritual Empowerment and Neutralizing Personal Chaos

The three main paths to spiritual development involve techniques and activities for enhancing the body/mind/spirit connection, reigning in negative impulses, and cultivating a positive mindset.

The First Path

The first path contains numerous and rather obvious articles; obvious at first glance, but excellent activities that will help fine-tune the body, mind, and spirit. When these activities are really acted on with sincerity and commitment over a period of time, not all at once, you can begin your own journey!

Meditation

Slow down and sit down. Find a quiet, private place, same time every day, once or twice a day; expand to seven days a week eventually. Sit on a floor mat (look up yoga and meditation positions in bookstores and libraries), blanket, or thick cushion; if you have a bad back or other physical problems, try a comfortable chair—always sitting with a straight spine. Breathe in through the nose, exhale through the nose. If it's more comfortable, inhale air to the bottom of the lungs, then exhale through the mouth, any way to gain comfort and calmness. Hold your breath for a count of ten slow seconds. Keep your eyes slightly closed. Think of nothing; if pictures or visions appear, let them. After several sessions and when you feel confident, expand the time of meditation to twenty minutes or longer. The purpose of meditation is to rest, find calmness, and quiet your mind. If you find that you want more, breathe in several sets with longer seconds. Visions and insights can occur when you are confident in this quiet-mind exercise.

Exercise

Every other day, either walk, jog, lift weights, do yoga or gi gong, practice tai chi, hike, swim, bicycle, or participate in team sports—anything that will loosen and strengthen muscles while clearing the mind. Fit your favorite exercise into your busy daily schedule. Frequency and duration are up to you. It's okay to work up a sweat; forget personal problems. Have a breath exchange with nature.

Diet

Avoid junk foods, go easy on red meats, eat lots of vegetables and fruits, and drink a lot of water during the day. Juices without added sugars are a substitute for soda pop. Don't drink anything with caffeine. If overweight, cut down on food intake; if badly underweight, build a better diet for strength and stamina without fats and sugars; if unsure, see a physician. Stay off drugs for bulking up.

Goal Setting

If you don't like your life or if you want to enrich it, set goals with time frames that are gradual and simple at first. Build on them, stick to them, and ask yourself what you've got to lose or what will you gain. You will have to decide for yourself about where you want to go or what your needs are. Research with friends, counselors, libraries, the Internet, or go into your mind. Be private with goals; write them down in a journal and revisit them weekly.

Volunteering

Helping others will help you. Everyone can spare time to work unpaid in people or animal assisting organizations; check writing is not volunteering. Personal satisfaction and positive ego gratification can result by helping; every city and town has an organization meant for you. Get involved!

Reading

By taking time to read books on subjects that interest you, or something you know nothing about, you will get pleasure while expanding your universe; this is a much better use of time than mindless situation comedies on television. And you can escape in stolen moments, while building a better vocabulary and creating a bank of personal knowledge.

Kindness

Practice doing nice things for family, friends, and perfect strangers. Kind words, errands, civility, and lending a helping hand are always right directions; mean it! This kindness also extends to animals. Be kind to yourself. The good, true self is open, honest, kind, and sincere. Loyalty and duty to others is a big plus.

Avoid Negatives

A difficult habit to break is gossiping and negative words; think positives for others as well as yourself. Keep a daily note pad, writing everything that you did that was negative (including thoughts); look at the notes and try not to repeat. If possible, turn negatives into positives; don't let negative karma be your companion. Only you will know for sure—especially if you believe in negative or positive karma; remember that negative thoughts are not good for anyone! It's hard, but train yourself to respond to life with serenity and the positive aspects.

Listen

Practice listening instead of talking; listen to the sounds of your environment, work, or home. By listening to others instead of using idle chatter and upmanship you will pick up thoughts and feelings of others, especially family and friends.

Mortality

Remember that you are indeed mortal; none of us knows the hour when our time is up on this fair planet. As has been previously mentioned, we will spend far more time over there than here. Do good deeds for others now and also for yourself, keeping in mind that preparation for the final journey is also an important step in spiritual development. Ask yourself how you want to be remembered. Have you made a difference? Will you be carrying light or heavy baggage to the otherside?

The Second Path

The second path to personal spiritual discovery and enlightenment is borrowed from Buddhism and needs no interpretation:

- Do not kill.
- Do not steal.
- Do not be greedy.
- Do not tell a lie.
- Do not be ignorant.
- Do not talk about other's faults.

- Do not elevate yourself by criticizing others.

- Do not be stingy.

- Do not be angry.

Of course, there seems to be a lot of "do nots," but as previously mentioned, the journey to spiritual rebirth and discovery is not an easy road. We must rein in our negative impulses. It is important to realize we don't have to live as a monk or the perfect human. You must keep your mind strong and focused, combining activities, deeds, and compassion without becoming rigid, inflexible, and stagnant. Stay in the mainstream, keeping a positive flow of energy coursing and vibrating through your mind and spirit. Any well-grounded person knows what values, passions, personality, strengths and weaknesses, ambitions and goals are best for him or her and do not conflict with society's artificial mores and demands.

The Third Path

The third path to spiritual liberation is thinking, feeling, believing, and practicing a positive mind set, which we will call the gentle spirit.

- Keep emotions and anger under control.

- Listen to the other person's point of view.

- Meet adversity with humor.

- Avoid a sense of superiority.

- Avoid blaming others for personal adversities.

- Avoid physical confrontations.

- Be honest in love and sex.

- Be respectful of people, animals, and the environment.

- Leave a difficult and strained situation in peace.

- Cultivate and celebrate a fondness for art, music, literature and the higher self—of all cultures.

- Remain open to innovation and discovery.

- Avoid greed, envy, and jealousy.

- Treat the body well by exercising, proper diet, and refusing the impurities of drugs and excessive alcohol.

The journey we all share in seeking spiritual unfoldment can be difficult to maneuver, but if we are truly interested in reducing the power of the demons that hound, then we have to sort out what is best. There are indeed many "Dos," but what if we never try?

At first glance these three paths seem familiar, are common knowledge, and perhaps they seem impossible to achieve, but on a second scrutiny they appear as one. We know too much time is wasted on negative energy than is expended on positive energy, but the misuse of uncommitted energy (apathy, indifference, and laziness) is even more harmful. If we desire a sane personal life, want a productive working life and an abundant social life, then the attempt at reinventing our lives is a paramount concern. Faith and belief for change is hollow unless action is taken.

Surviving a life that has more downs than ups is difficult. Like energy does attract like energy, and the energy forces of the universe found through personal trial and error can be harnessed into establishing harmony and balance only with effort. In a nutshell, spirituality can help us live a better, more satisfying and fulfilling life, especially when we let go of mental limitations. We all want to take control of our lives, but this cannot be undertaken until we override the negatives. A life, a successful and healthy one, combines honest self-cultivation in mind, body, and energy. Our spiritual self has a lot to do with this. Action and movement coupled with focus opens any door.

We are blessed, some more than others, with free will; we feel, we think, and we act. Spirituality becomes a philosophy about living. Moralizing about spirituality can result in a great waste of time and energy. As a popular advertising slogan states, "Just do it!"

Since our life on earth is a schoolhouse, why not enrich our studies in preparation for the great and final transition? Instead of being a confused human with a confused soul, shouldn't we try to value our life's journey? At times we live disconnected and anxious. A spiritual existence requires that we live to the fullest, that we surrender to the excruciating power of love for others and ourselves, where responsibility, passion, and commitment lead to a spiritual trail. In the real world of our present experience we will inevitably encounter joy, some pain, and perhaps opportunities that wait for us when we take action.

We then become more loving and giving to others, further discovering that people are essentially good and kind. Perhaps we can even rid ourselves of that feeling of alienation and disconnection our anthill society of overpopulation imposes on us. The panacea for anxiety, tension, and stress comes from a reinvention and introduction to our spiritual side, an uplifting of our soul.

A Personal Reconnection

Recently, to reconnect and infuse myself with the spiritual side I had somewhat put aside, I went on a retreat at a Zen center. I participated in the stark and simple rituals of zazen (sit and meditate) and listened earnestly to numerous teishos (lectures on life experiences by the Zen master); primed by very simple food, rituals, incense, bells, and silence to clear and uplift my mind. With problems somewhat settled, especially concerning dharma aspects, I felt ready and refreshed to face the world. I revisited many pleasant memories as a brash young U.S. Navy sailor stationed in Japan, where I first had been exposed to Zen's special meditation techniques and philosophy. Out of this recent and past reconnection, I again found the release of tension and the relearning of contemplative prayer and meditation.

We all need a contemplative retreat at times and a temporary withdrawal from life's demands. We need to connect or reconnect with the spirituality that is in all of us. We can manipulate our egos to positive advantage. Meditation, prayer, good thoughts and deeds can assist us in knocking down our demons to manageable size, and our short time in this planet schoolhouse can be excellent preparation for the next great adventure that all of us will undertake.

The Shadows

Dealing with stress and its partner anxiety can become a major obstacle in the construction of a spiritual life. Listed on page 77 are some of the physical and mental consequences of not overcoming or coping with stress. How many do you have?

Fatigue	Diarrhea	Headaches
Insomnia	Constipation	Colds
Irritability	Indigestion	Flu
Anger	Overeating	Excessive drinking
Nervousness	Depression	Pill popping and drugs
Aggression	Forgetfulness	Poor concentration
Poor self-esteem	Poor appetite	Low sex drive

At some point, perhaps numerous times, a few of these stress-induced factors have gotten out of control in our lives, eventually leading to periods of antisocial behavior. It would be a ridiculous assumption to state that living a perfect spiritual life will banish or mitigate the total impact of stress and its symptoms, but we can surely try by taking life a little easier and identifying our demons.

It is hard to keep the perspective that we do have a contract with life and that a complete or total attempt should be undertaken that could reduce or remove the unpleasant aspects of stress and its ugly children. Coping can be an initial thrust, but day-to-day depression, fear, anger, jealousy, bad moods, anxiety, and physical and emotional complaints should be eliminated before permanent damage is done. We must refuse to believe that behind every cloud is an even darker cloud.

Many prescriptions have been offered to eliminate stress: mental and physical activity, proper diet, career changing, sleep, vacations, relationships—the list is endless. Optimism and love appear to be clear antidotes. Some individuals practice stress removal and reduction by keeping away from unpleasant noises, avoidance of confrontations, exercise, feng shui (furniture and environment arrangement), soothing music, journal writing, aromatherapy, and a million other things. If it works, then why not?

The reason stress is being hit repeatedly in this chapter is because it is one of the principal enemies to self-actualization and spiritual development. By removing skepticism and stress, adding understanding and commitment to the three paths, sprinkled with additional information *and* taking action with Freud's "keys," you can become a spiritual being—yes, even in the "real" world.

Mediums and mystics, if they are to deal honestly with society, themselves, and the otherside, should, as much as possible, be removed and apart from the boundaries that hinder the mainstream of any society. They look beyond this dimension, seeing into other dimensions. Mediums can be just as susceptible to stress as the next person while struggling with maintaining the aspects of being a spiritual being and like the rest of us, be sidetracked from the three paths. They also know the basic truth that spirituality and walking the path in earnest will lead to clearer and frequent visions, especially contact with the departed.

In our locomotion-driven culture, there comes a time when we want to jump off a train that is uncomfortable and going nowhere. Many of us are confused or afraid to leave the train. When is the right time? Obviously, spiritual preparation and revamping can ready an individual for the big jump, but only when that individual finally realizes he or she is tired of being a confused human with a confused soul. Tranquility and harmony are not yet in that individual's vocabulary. Deficits in soul health, mental health, and physical health are tough situations to attack and shouldn't be relegated to the back burner.

Action finally occurs when we grow thoroughly tired of the void in our lives and when we can no longer hide from pressures in the quiet zone that we have constructed, physical or emotional, which no longer seems to be the place of safe refuge.

From television, newspapers, books, and magazines, we learn about people who have escaped their personal demons by commitment to selfless deeds and works for others—becoming "givers" instead of "takers." Some of our friends have become connected with helping in their communities. Have they become spiritual beings through compassion? They do seem to have one thing in common— "happy hearts." Perhaps through some sort of epiphany they became givers. Having grown tired of drifting down a raging river with no mooring or lifeline, they decided to take control of their spiritual lives. They have empowered themselves. These wonderful souls have prepared the road for us, especially if we seek them out and learn through their discoveries.

Spiritually, our lives do not come with a money-back guarantee of satisfaction.

"If you want a guarantee, buy a toaster."
—FROM *THE ROOKIE*, (1990 CLINT EASTWOOD MOVIE)

Establishing an Equilibrium of Harmony

In just one day per month you can learn more about your inner self through listening openly and honestly to those around you. You can even accrue a personal bank account filled with positive deposits of intimacy, concentration, and connection. Think of it, one day per month of simplicity—lower blood pressure and time for yourself and those you love, time to take control instead of being controlled, a retreat from the demands of the world.

At first glance it looks impossible to take or steal a day and escape to the mountains or beach for yourself. But you can even do this great escape at home in a trial run. Who wants to be away from the frenzy of civilization for twenty-four hours anyway? Maybe adding a few months to your life—who would want to do that? Time for yourself? A quality life instead of a quantified life? Listed below is a sample of how you can tailor a stolen day and achieve harmony and intimacy with yourself and your environment.

The No's

- No errands
- No cooking: order in or take out; lay in snacks or meals cooked beforehand. No restaurants or bars
- No shopping centers
- No driving (or as little as possible)
- No telephones
- No movies, television, radio, newspapers, or magazines
- No computer, Palm Pilot, electronic games
- No talking or thinking about work

The Do's

- Sleep late
- Meditate or pray

- Play cards, chess, games

- Do crossword puzzles

- Read books, none work related

- Take showers or long baths

- Listen to "easy" music

- Use candles in evening instead of lights

- Have unhurried sex

The purpose of this one-day-per-month simplicity program is to expend as little energy as possible, and to become grounded and centered. The key is to rest and let your mind slow down during this personal retreat. Share conversation and intimate moments with spouse, mate, and children—and listen! Perhaps if you keep at it, you will discover, reconfirm, or reestablish your inner spirit.

When you become comfortable with following this basic list, add gardening, hiking, walking, fishing, swimming, museums, art galleries, and picnics—not all at once, of course. A hint for the success of this simplicity-intimacy exercise is to remain technology free (somewhat), while banking as much positive energy as possible. It's only for one day a month, and imagine the joy of finding that "certain something" that is your inner spirit, and a reconnection with the simple pleasures of life. You can eventually expand this stolen time into a few more days a month.

Summary of Achieving an Abundant Spiritual Life

Some individuals seem to thrive as the star of their own personal melodrama or soap opera. Surviving daily catastrophes and disasters is not living. We are searching for an abundant life comprised of balance and harmony.

Controlling "hang-ups" that occurred in the past can be a difficult proposition; many times we carry the scars of past events, but closure is imperative in order to have a harmonious balance in our present life. Three things we must realize:

- The past is done; we leave this ancient history where it belongs—in the past.

- We are living the *now*.

- The future is not here yet.

If we are not to repeat the mistakes of the past, we must learn to connect with life now, and with balance and reality. Success is relative to what we consider failure. We can use our mistakes to learn to get over it and move along, especially if we lose the ugly aspects of an ego's defense mechanism: anger, hostility, aggression, mistrust, and withdrawal. We need to reach for a serendipitous mixture of love, intimacy, sensitivity, and affection to focus on what's best in life. A close examination of our attitudes indicates that we do indeed have a grand connection with life, be it positive or negative.

The Emphasis of Spiritual Connection

- Accept yourself and others

- Be open to change

- Know where you are going

- Listen

- Learn to love your body and mind

- Learn to love

- Quality of life instead of quantity

- Participate in life

- Be active in mind and body

- Don't let time run out; move, move!

- Connect with the universe/cosmos/God

- Develop genuine compassion for others

- Handle disappointments

- Control negative emotions
- Develop positive relationships
- Meditate daily
- Live every day as if it was your last

The aware person is one who knows nothing remains static. Change is the bottom line of life. Obviously, the contents of this chapter have been simplified in order for you to take immediate action. Most of these topics are repeats and rephrases; many of us know that new directions and a reinvention of our personalities are needed from time to time. Some of them could be a struggle to incorporate into our lives. If we can make changes, all the better; if sacrifice is needed for change, perhaps this can be a good thing—a testing of our fiber. Action in attempting change can only help lighten baggage, which is much easier to carry than heavy trunks. What do you think?

In this so-called real world of our existence, we realize it is keenly important how we play the game. The "tools" we use in playing this game of life are critical to our survival if we are to flourish in this superficial existence. We are the true guardians of our souls.

A Few Words on Soul Power

Our soul, if you accept the premise of a soul, is what makes us animated and alive. The soul is the very essence and stuff of our being, containing accrued thoughts, memories, actions, feelings, experiences, and accumulated knowledge. It is the sum total of our personality. It is our spirituality. It is a separate function from our physical body and survives our physical death. We will be either happy or miserable in this life and the next one because of what we fed it.

We have to occasionally ignore or distance ourselves from the spirit of our times and the chaos that surrounds us, focusing instead on what we believe is moral and right, not only to ourselves but to others. There is and always has been a dark side lurking in the human condition. Somehow, in some way, many of us will manage to leave this life by having done the right thing. The Golden Rule, "Do unto others as you would have others do unto you," is very applicable.

Living in a depersonalized, aggressive, hostile, yet exciting and loving environment pulls us every which way—but we can manage to neutralize the negative aspects through the development and nurturing of our own spirituality. Even when we open the door to receive our personal brand of spirituality, we still have to choose to either walk through that door or to close it. It's a personal decision. We have so many choices in life; we know we have to choose wisely, especially when it comes to such an important thing as our immortal soul.

Things are not always apparent on the surface, so we must always question the reality that is served us and look deeper into our being. We know our mission is to seek the passion, joy, and beauty of this life; to create a transformation in our life; and on this path of discovery to obtain self-empowerment, self-awareness, self-awakening, and self-enlightenment. When we step back from the chaos around us and in us, we are on the way to attaining balance and harmony. It is very possible in this search that we will find the social interaction, confidence, and well-balanced self-esteem that will help us reach a rewarding life.

It has been thought, even prophesied, that the quest for spirituality and living as a spiritual being is the new religion of this millennium. Presently, there seems to be a growing movement to break away from the chokehold of materialism and disconnection. Perhaps this is why the influence of Eastern religions and thoughts is now making such rapid inroads in Western societies. It should be an interesting millennium.

Angel in the Street

About four years ago I met an angel—I'm convinced of it. A busy time of day—lunchtime, on a very crowded, open street mall in downtown Denver, feeling very depressed over a bad morning at work—she came to me.

Waiting for a corner stoplight to turn green, I for some reason looked across the next street. There in the crowded street, I saw this tall woman, elegantly dressed in a two-piece, cream-colored suit with a small picture hat. She was looking directly at me with a smile that lit up her face.

When the light changed, somehow she was next to me as I crossed the street. Her "angelic" face glowed with a strange radiance, accented with a stunning smile. Speaking softly, she said, "Don't be depressed, there are far more things to take delight in. This is meaningless." Well, not sure if it was a come on, I said lamely, "You're right." She then said, "I have to go to Minneapolis in a few minutes to help a grieving mother survive the death of a son who hanged himself today. That's real depression." I stopped in my tracks to look at her more closely.

She continued, I swear it, to radiate a beauty and calmness that seemed to wash over me. I said a thank you, wanting to say more, but the crowd was jostling us into moving. I looked over at her—she was gone!

I looked up and down the street, even looking into the windows of nearby shops, but I didn't see her.

That afternoon, I felt charged at work, getting rid of overdue paperwork that had languished in my in-basket, all the while feeling a calmness and inner peace that I hadn't felt in a very long time. My depression had evaporated. For a week I dreamed of angels in my sleep—while remembering her advice and radiant smile.

This story can be explained away by the skeptical, but to the receptive and open-minded, angels and spirit guides do appear when needed in times of distress. I know what I saw and experienced.

Angels are very adept at coaxing spirituality from the buried recesses of our mind, and bringing out the best in us. As a follow-up to this story, I decided to retire from my job in order to preserve my integrity and character. I haven't been unhappy since. Supernatural forces can and do make a difference in our lives if we let them.

The Grand Conclusion 6

Only by much searching and mining are gold and diamonds obtained, and man can find every truth connected with his being if he will dig deep into the mind of his soul.

—JAMES ALLEN

The Grand Conclusion

Our preoccupation with materialism is a "now" thing. Breaking from the collecting of toys and prestige is seldom chanced— we might lose out in the race. Our possessions have taken a life of their own, holding us for ransom. Nonetheless, there is still a certain feeling, an almost supernatural urge, tugging at us, whispering that there is more to life than the accumulation of objects and status.

When we stroll along a restless seashore to momentarily escape the stress of the city and our frantic existence, subconsciously or consciously seeking to put balance back in our life, even if only for an hour, we are attempting to regain the original spirituality that once charged the passions of our childhood and young adulthood, and we are left with a lingering sense of frustration. We know it's there, our spirituality—somewhere close, ever elusive, and as difficult to catch as lightning in a bottle.

Each time we walk through a park, tend a garden, fish in a lake, hike a verdant forest or gasp at the beauty of serene snow-capped mountains, we sense that once again we've touched the essence of our soul.

Perhaps for a few stolen minutes we contemplate the short lives of dead animals in the road while we dash to work. Maybe on our walk through a placid park we again encounter a dead bird or squirrel, maybe this time wondering if it had a soul and went on to some sort of animal paradise. Smugly, we are comforted in the bosom of our weekend organized religions, sure that we will matriculate to a heaven when our time comes. Then our thoughts quickly flash back to Aunt Mary's funeral, where we briefly held tortured thoughts on mortality, a most unpleasant subject for humans, which we quickly shelved for later consideration, because Aunt Mary was sick and old, after all.

We may sometimes feel a cobweb caress our face when there isn't one; have tingles at the back of the neck, feel a soft puff of air in the ears when there is no breeze, or just know that something is stroking our hair. Or we may abruptly awaken from sleep holding the fragmented pieces of a dream in which death took the stage and where we or people we know were the central actors.

All of these things, from walks on the beach to observing dead animals, feeling strange sensations, or experiencing troubled dreams, become imbedded in the back of our subconscious, and with the right physical and mental stimulus, they can suddenly be yanked to the foreground, and we wonder why. Mediums call these physical and mental occurrences "spirit whispers." Spirit whispers are the stuff of premonitions, intuitions, Extrasensory Perceptions (ESP), and clairvoyance, attributes we are born with, know well as children, and ignore as adults, but which lie dormant within our psyche.

These whispers remain in fallow most of our lives. But we know instinctively that life is a gift, not a right, and that it must not be squandered. Uneasiness and stress tend to push us to a yearning for comfort and release and a search for inner peace and meaning in the war for our soul.

We can all become winners in this soul war through spiritual enlightenment. Consider all hints of self-discovery and death preparation that come to you via the spiritual path as gifts from our friends on the otherside, who recognize that all beings in the universe are part of the great cosmic chain, in which there is no beginning and no end. Constructing and exploring new approaches to life and the understanding of mortality commences with the discovery of personal spirituality. And this discovery eventually leads to a more perfect integration of life and thought, now and when the time comes for the transition from the earth plane.

In the Material World

Think of a world where there is no disease, anger, and hate; no wars, killings, hunger, physical or emotional abuse, a world where virtue is rewarded and morality is the true path of enlightenment; where the earth and the environment is beautiful beyond any known description; where all creatures are treated with respect and love. Imagine a planet filled with so much love that it almost hurts. Think of a world where megacorporations, governments, politicians and officials, professional athletes and entertainers play second fiddle to a loving, caring, and sharing populace that manages its own character development and survival—unfettered.

Alas, the real world is what we have to deal with and attempt to survive in. Nonetheless we still must exert an effort to make this world a better place, ignoring the flying brickbats. Could this perfection of character and environment be beyond reach because we're placed in the universe to learn? Is planet Earth one of many schoolhouses scattered throughout the known universe where we are located temporarily in order to learn how to overcome the adversities of life in preparation for that other place?

One thing we do learn from the very material nature of our great universe allows us to be well assured that our personality survives our physical demise. Our physical body decays with the cessation of life; however, we know that decaying energy-matter takes a renewed life in a different form, as the first law of physical thermodynamics dictates.

Those different forms show up in indirect or direct sightings and by sensing with that certain feeling ghosts, apparitions, and spirits, guaranteeing that something rather exciting occurs beyond our physical death. There are just too many thousands of reported cases over thousands of years not to believe in the continuance of the human personality.

Spirit communication through mediums, visits to the living by spirits, Near Death Experiences, and Astral Projections to the otherside—or a parallel universe—should at least pose some valid questions to science and the skeptical, and perhaps even offer proof that they are failing to understand many of the key facets concerning the basic nature of the universe. It is not a matter of self-deception to believe in the idea that there is an evolution of the soul; it's not even a matter of belief versus hard evidence, because the universe allows no total destruction of matter or energy.

Interestingly enough, a September 2001 *Scientific American* poll extracted from the Gallup Organization and Nielsen Media Research, found out from those polled the following:

Phenomenon	Percent Who Believe
Psychic or spiritual healing	54%
Extrasensory perception	50%
Haunted houses	42%
Ghosts or spirits	38%
Telepathy	36%
Extraterrestrials visited earth	33%
Communication with the dead	28%
Astrology	28%
Reincarnation	25%

This poll is cited only to offer a basic index showing that some individuals have divergent views from the accepted norm. Actually, these poll results could be considered startling in their overall findings: the results do indicate that independent thinking is taking place outside the box and that questioning of the accepted norm is occurring. Perhaps the population in general is seeking or yearning for alternate views and solutions to unanswered questions.

Throwing in another poll, from the August 2002, Harvard Health Letter, medical researchers at a major hospital in St. Louis, Missouri, reported that 7 of 30 (23 percent) cardiac-arrest survivors interviewed had near-death experiences during the arrest. In these experiences they described feelings of peacefulness, calmness, lack of fear, "detachment from the body," and "timelessness."

We either believe or don't believe in life after death. The signs that we do survive are everywhere if we will only take a few moments to look, listen, and feel. Science offers us indirect evidence that we do survive because we are made of the same indestructible substance of our universe—energy and matter—but more than that, those of us who've caught glimpses into the invisible realm know there is so much that we don't know or understand. It becomes asinine to scoff at the possibilities. A skeptic believes in what he can see, feel, or touch, bolstered by some misplaced need for pseudointellectualism. The skeptic, by ignoring or castigating others who are concerned with the matter of life after death, limits his field of vision, thereby lessening his own spirituality and growth, and definitely their impartiality.

By keeping an open mind an individual lessens rigidity of thinking and belief, thereby staying aware to the possibility that anything and everything is possible in our universe—what is accepted as scientific fact today can become a discarded theory tomorrow. It's our choice to take the high road or the low road, knowing full well that we do have the option of using our free will.

For certain, no single approach, such as Eastern mysticism, Western philosophy, spiritual empowerment, or traditional religion, is able to reveal all the survival skills and techniques for living this life, and certainly not for the experiences waiting us in the final "Great Mystery." But we can discover many personal insights when we drop dogmatic skepticism and learn to look, listen, and explore, coaching our minds to become less rigid and more receptive when questioning accepted assumptions.

There is an old quip, Zen I believe, which says, "Before enlightenment, you chop wood and carry water; after enlightenment, you still chop wood and carry water." Let it be added that with enlightenment, tasks and burdens are undertaken with more joy and purpose, that material possessions and status become secondary to the ability to thrive, love, and adapt. We can reach that certain triumph and resilience of spirit in a reinvention of self, which will allow us to live happily while preparing us for the final journey, our grand conclusion.

The Most Important Part of this Book— the Moment of Our Death, a Rehash

When anything "dies," we must believe it to be not death,
but change only, for neither the soul or the body suffers annihilation.
—GIORDANO BRUNO

Obviously this book would never be complete without comments on our spirit guides, those eternal beings who greet and escort us through our transformation to the otherside. As human beings we've been mysteriously tapped for stardom out of all the life forms on our planet. Through millions of years of our evolutionary struggle, assisted by the unseen forces of our vast universe, and for the most obscure and exciting reasons yet unknown, we've been granted the boon of an immortal soul.

It is a monumental occurrence to be able to meet these guides while we live (when we are open or in need), and it's most certainly an earth-shattering experience to be greeted by them during the stages of crossing over. Imagine, we are guided and protected by these angels of the universe while alive, as well as escorted and aided by them in the great beyond!

As has been previously touched upon in this book, we all have a spirit guide or guardian angel, perhaps even a spirit team, attending to our needs during crises. Some of them stay with us from birth to death, and others become special substitutes depending on our spiritual growth—or lack of spiritual growth—and development. Many of us are able to sense a presence, especially when we are undergoing periods of dire physical or emotional distress. Also, during meditation or a relaxed state we are particularly open and receptive for their contact. We tap into their presence through intuition, dreams, and best of all, a personal meeting.

We have the free will to either follow or thwart their guidance and assistance; it's always a matter of personal choice. Our guides can exert a powerful and amazing influence on us, depending on how open and spiritual we are. The development of that "certain feeling" is an innate mechanism given to us at birth. Children, with their trusting innocence, can see and talk to these guides, not yet having learned to block them out as adults do. But if we remain receptive to them through the years of our lives, we can avoid many of the pitfalls that seemingly hound us. On the other hand, if the dark side is dominant in our personality, we can be left open to negative influences, possibly even attracting lower forms of spirit.

When we die, we lose our physical body; the etheric, or astral, body—our soul's energy force—becomes the vehicle of transportation. We then meet a guide who takes us through a "life review" process. This life review has been likened to the final stages of drowning, with life events flashing rapidly through the mind, similar to undergoing the Near Death Experience. The life review process appears to be accomplished in a split second.

Everything you've ever seen, heard, smelled, experienced in any way is reviewed with little or no judgment being rendered. When you're with the guide(s) expect to be startled, elated, depressed, shocked, or in a state of bliss; these emotions do continue until the earth bonds are finally slipped. You will cry, deny, and gush with emotional release and elation—maybe even shame, because it's all part of the experience.

In ancient Egypt, according to the "Book of the Dead," the first step in the journey to immortality began with the soul (heart) being placed on a double scale and weighed against the feather of truth and purity; if the soul was heavier than the feather, the deceased was either eaten by a denizen of the underworld or was sent back to the earth plane as a haunting spirit (ghost). If the soul was not found wanting in purity and good deeds and was in balance with the feather, it was sent on its way to begin the next phase of immortality.

The shock of death, whether expected or not, and the subsequent and inevitable transfiguration, is in the realization that you've entered eternity, which can be a rather unsettling experience. Some won't take this transmigration or transition passage willingly or smoothly because of disbelief, detachment, commitment to lifetime activities, shock, remorse, and fear of the unknown; these souls will stay earthbound or suspended in a state of non-movement (limbo?).

Those who tried to do their best for self and others while retaining their spirit of joy and desire to move on to higher aspirations can enter the transitional plane of a Summerland.

After this life review process is concluded, a short period of bliss (earth days or even weeks) is spent with a spirit guide during a period of orientation. This period of the soul's journey allows the deceased to become acclimated to the fact that they are indeed dead—their earth life as they knew it is really over. Questions are later answered and demonstrated in Summerland, such as how movement and communications are accomplished, and adjustments are made, such as getting used to not having a physical body. In this new world, it must be remembered, we still retain much of our earth personality, and we must learn how to drop the negative aspects. The happier and more settled we become, the quicker we transition out of confusion and bewilderment.

The physical form taken is a mass of energy, likened to small globes of white light, similar to the spirit guides being met. At times, to place us at ease, the guides appear in the forms they had when (and if) they were alive on this earth plane or the universe.

Restated . . .

- The earthly laws of physics cannot define the astral dimensions as a theory or reality, nor can they offer proof either way of existence—at least not yet.

- Strangely, we are energy in an invisible, immaterial world.

- In death, our soul holds the sum total of our personality, memories, thoughts, will and desires, actions, and all emotions.

- There is no heaven or hell in death as we've been taught, only what we expect; we can view our new journey in fear or with excitement.

- The entire life review process is nonjudgmental—facts and actions stand alone.

- We are the sole judge and jury on how we spent our life, thus our degree of spirituality weighs heavily in the balance of our soul's direction. Our guide(s) during this life review will not act as judge and jury.

- We have the option to make a smooth transmigration to the otherside or not, whether to stay earth-bound or to move on.

- When we lose our physical body, our etheric, or astral, body becomes our vehicle of transportation. All physical infirmities are also left behind if desired.

- Perhaps it's best to look on life as a grand illusion and secondly as a school for returning "home" (eventually), with information for astral upgrades.

- Reincarnation is a spirit option for returning to the earth plane for further experiences and improvement of character and spirituality.

We all will take a turn in waltzing with death—the dance card is never filled, the waltz never through. There are so many tools we can borrow from the universe's limitless toolbox to coach reason and lessen panic for the "big" transformation. It's always a good thing to ever enjoy this magnificent life to its fullness, to "be in the moment," but when questions crop up about what's next after our life's final moment, then the medium can help alleviate some of these anxieties.

So, as you can readily see from reading this book, the greatest secrets of this clairvoyant-medium, or any clairvoyant for that matter, are in attaining an honest and hopeful spirituality with a firm belief in an afterlife. Achieving a joyful, giving, caring, loving, and sharing spirituality in this life, our magnificent souls will make the final transition, the transmigration to the otherside fearlessly and full of the hope and excitement of a new journey.

Meditational Exercises

The Importance of Meditation

With the aid of intense, focused meditation you can enter the portals of spirit communication and contact, healing, and prophecy. Through trance or an altered state of consciousness, the barriers of our world can be lessened, much as an astronaut entering outer space drops the restraints and pull of gravity—freedom!

Dare to dream and believe. With purpose, focus, and refinement of technique, coupled with expectation and heavy doses of belief, you can possibly alleviate stress, develop personal insight, and garner sight beyond the standard senses. Without meditation there is no mediumship.

It's All in the Technique

- Wear loose, comfortable clothing.

- Pick a quiet space, or better yet, a room with a closed door.

- Close windows if it's noisy outside.

- No noise allowed! Disconnect telephones, turn off pagers and cell phones, the television, radio, stereo, etc. Eventually, with experience, the stereo loaded with CDs of soft instrumental music or nature-environmental sounds might assist your total trance immersion.

- Banish distractions like pets, children, or whatever, that will require your attention in these stolen moments away from the world. (When you become a pro at meditation, distractions will be easy to ignore.)

- Sit on the floor on a comfortable blanket, pillows, or mat. A comfortable, not-easy-to-sleep-in chair will also do.

- Sit with your spine straight up.

- Face a blank wall, removing such distractions as mirrors or pictures.

- Relax by deep breathing; inhale deep breaths through your nose, exhaling through your mouth. Relax and relax! Feel the air go down to the bottom of your stomach, then slowly up through your lungs, and out through your mouth. Deep breathe until you feel a tingling sensation in your legs and arms; you might even feel light-headed, but keep the breathing exchange going. Relax! Don't cheat! Keep breathing. Don't think of anything; let your mind become blank—don't rush—keep your mind blank.

If you experience "mind chatter," then let it be; you can't simply turn off your mind the first time you try—but you will be able to eventually, if you continue to practice.

The other method of meditation breathing is in through nose and out through nose—any method to make you calm and refreshed. You could try another popular posture method too, which is to lie on the floor, feet flat on floor with knees up. Breath exchange is up to you—sets of deep breathing for thirty seconds (holding), expelling, then repeat, or whatever you feel comfortable with, depending on your lung capacity—never be uncomfortable in posture or breathing method.

Frequency of meditation is up to you too, but once a day is best—your special quiet time—commencing with twenty minutes a day, increasing to as long as you feel it work; some do meditation twice a day.

Remember, meditation is listening, for relaxation and calmness, as well as to receive visions and communication. When you feel you are relaxed and your mind is open to receive, you can use the three following initial exercises; later, with experience, you can build your own "scripts."

The Green Room

With your eyes closed, sitting in a comfortable position, while breathing steadily, count backwards slowly from thirty to zero—visualize these numbers. See yourself walking alongside a calm ocean beach in the moonlight. It's warm outside, with a soft breeze bringing the delightful smell of the salty ocean in through your nostrils. You can hear and feel the crunch of the cool sandy beach on your tingling bare feet. You stop momentarily and look to your right, seeing a small cliff not more than fifteen yards away. You walk slowly to the cliff with purpose, seeing a shining brass doorknob in the moonlight. You approach the door, place your hand on the knob, and twist it open—you notice the door you expected to find is wide and high enough to walk through.

The door opens silently with no effort. Instinctively your left hand finds a light switch next to the doorway, and you flick it on and are amazed at the sight—a large green room, covered from floor to ceiling in some sort of green feltlike material; everything is green, including a raised, circular platform in the middle of the room.

On the platform is a green easel holding a large, very ornate, green plaster picture frame holding a large green canvas. Next to the easel is a small, green table with a paint can and a one-inch brush. The paint can contains brilliant, metallic gold paint. You pick up the brush and commence painting the ornate picture frame, slowly at first, then with quick purpose. The paint glides on the picture frame until the green color is completely covered by gold paint.

You look at the green canvas and decide to paint it with the glittering gold paint. The gold paint quickly covers the green canvas. You stand back for a few moments to admire your handiwork, and then your mind takes over.

You concentrate on the golden canvas and suddenly the questions you have or the solutions you want, seem to appear on the canvas. They can appear as words or animated figures or objects. Do you see the universe or somebody that crossed over? Is that your spirit guide? Do you see the spot where you lost something? What is it you want? To see future events? You let your thoughts mentally paint the canvas. There are *no* limits. You might even see movement and hear voices from the pictures your mind has created.

After you're satisfied, you decide to leave your personal Green Room, intending to come back soon, knowing that your questions, problems, and wishes will take a life of their own, waiting for your next visit and the painting of the frame and the canvas; the Green Room might even appear in your dreams.

You walk out of the room, turn off the lights and close the door. Walking along the beach you decide its time to return to the world. You face the ocean and slowly count, this time from zero to thirty.

You're back. You feel refreshed and relaxed now—calm and in control; you feel you have some of the answers, feel a release, or know the direction you must take; in any case, you now know where you can go—every time—to see and to know.

Each time you go back to the private Green Room in your own personal universe, you must repaint the picture frame and canvas in metallic gold paint, because your thoughts and desires require time to materialize through this "physical exertion."

Good visions with this exercise!

The Blue Adobe Hut

You are now comfortably sitting; the breathing exercise has calmed you, and your mind is still. You eagerly await your temporary withdrawal from the chaotic world, knowing that when you return you will be refreshed and calm—and having the answers.

Counting slowly backward from thirty to zero, you visualize the numbers from your closed eyes and calm mind. Your breathing comes easy, breathing in through the nose, exhaling quietly through the mouth; all is quiet around you, and you feel a sense of anticipation.

You find yourself in a desert, and looking around in all directions, you take in the beauty of the landscape. The rich, red soil, stunted pinion pine trees; the Yucca in bloom with a delicate fragrance emitting from the white-yellow flowers. The blue hue of the cloudless sky seems to be unnatural in color. The day is warm, not hot, and the air seems to be in a vacuum with no breeze.

Walking to an almost dried-up creek you notice a small adobe hut with a thatched roof next to the creek. You enter the doorless hut, and in the pleasantly cool and dark room, you find the hut's floor covered with Navajo blankets and pillows. In one corner of the room you see a plain pottery bowl with lightly burning incense. The fragrance appears to be a mixture of sage and cedar wood, smelling sweet and somehow relaxing.

Sitting on the rug and multicolored pillows, you notice two deep pottery dishes, one filled with dark blue paint and the other with yellow paint. You rise, taking one of the two brushes next to the paint pots and rapidly paint the walls in dark blue; the paint glides on, requiring only one coat—without any dripping on the floor of the hut and your hands.

You stand back to admire your handiwork and the radiant shade of blue covering the walls. Then, without any hesitation, you pick up the other brush and rapidly dab yellow spots on all four corners of the blue walls; again no splatters or problems with the yellow paint bleeding into the blue paint. In seconds you complete your handiwork.

Sitting again on the comfortable floor of soft pillows, you take in the fragrance of the incense and the beauty of the colored walls. You immediately notice the yellow dabs of color have formed a star chart of a night sky. Staring at the wall in front of you, you suddenly feel drawn into the depth and textures of the universe you've just created.

The stars seem to move—and to hold you—your body feels light with the stars' motion. One of the stars seems to be growing much larger than the rest and becomes enormous as it absorbs you, yes, absorbs you while you become one with the universe. Your mind stills as you hear distant voices and see things. You know somehow that there are no constraints or boundaries as you meet individuals— past, present, or future beings—you know that you can visit places here or over there; there are no limits. Your mind knows what you want and so you let it guide you in this moment of peace and exploration.

Later, after you find what you are seeking, you are back in the blue adobe hut, feeling refreshed and at peace. You rise from the floor, go through the doorway and walk through the enchantment of the dry, warm, and fresh desert landscape. You pause from walking and slowly count from zero to thirty—it's time to return to the other world!

The Rainbow

The simple rainbow meditation exercise requires a strong mind for visualization, which becomes achieved through familiarity with the colors of the rainbow and repetition. It requires no countdown and is simple to do. The benefits of this self-hypnotic exercise are multifold: visions, alleviation of stress, and tuning your psychic abilities, and it can be used anywhere.

Picture yourself sitting on the top of a lush, green hill over-looking a steep valley filled with groves of trees, with the floor of the valley being carpeted in brightly colored flowers. A soft, misty rain has concluded, and everything is cool but not cold. You feel invigorated by the surroundings, pausing to breathe in the cool regenerating air—slowly in, slowly out. Suddenly, an incredibly brilliant rainbow appears in the blue, mottled sky, when the sun emerges from behind pink and white billowing clouds. The rainbow seems to cover the valley.

You feel protected and safe while looking at the clouds and the majestic rainbow. Strangely, you can hear a soft buzzing sound coming from the rainbow, but the pleasant sound makes you feel alert and somehow safe. Looking at the intense colors of the rainbow, you start at the top color of the rainbow which is red, and *slowly* descend through the rest of the colors—orange, yellow, green, blue, indigo, and violet ("Roy G. Biv" is the best way to remember the colors of the rainbow).

You stay with each color until you feel the intensity and vibration of that color washing over your entire body. When you complete the first round of colors, do it again and again until you feel relaxed, calm, and expectant. Let your thoughts come through—hopefully with the completion of three rounds, you will feel good and receptive to visions.

Keep working on this simple meditational exercise. You can use the rainbow before going to bed or before the events of the day transpire. Some individuals use this exercise while walking, hiking, or in the shower or bathtub. In any case, this is a great stress buster of an exercise. As stated previously, the rainbow is an excellent approach for honing psychic abilities.

In Summary

These simple exercises, as you will see, are all great at reducing stress. Perhaps meditation will allow you to meet your demons of spiritual and psychological distress and banish them. You impose your own limits as to what you want to "see." I recommend you start out for only twenty minutes at a time, once a day, or at least every other day. You can practice them while in bed, but I guarantee you will fall asleep. I also strongly endorse your invoking the power of the White Light for protection against unwanted entities and bad influences.

With practice and trial and error—fighting your mind for control—you can usher in the gift of prophecy, meet your guardian angels and spirit guides, even experience an Out of the Body adventure. As I also mentioned, the protection of the White Light is always a needed shield. Remember, you need to see and feel a white mist that envelopes your entire body; you then ask this Godlike force to protect you from any evil or bad influence—before and after your meditation.

In any case, doses of practice, belief, and expectancy can assist you in achieving a mind-altering experience that will gain you steps in the development of your spirituality and personal insight into the workings of the universe and who you are.

Vision is the art of seeing things invisible.
—JONATHAN SWIFT

A Glossary of
Paranormal Terms

Akashic Records: The chronicles or library of the universe. According to Edgar Cayce, the cosmos holds a record of everything that has happened or will ever happen for every person ever born on this planet and every intelligent life form in the universe. Every physical action, emotion, deed, thought, health situation, and vibration is "recorded." This library of souls in the universe can almost be likened to predetermination and fate. Through intense meditation, a psychically disciplined individual can obtain personal soul information and records on past, present, and future reincarnation.

Angels: Heavenly souls—with or without wings, depending on what form we want them to appear. They act as guardians or spirit guides for all of us; many are with us throughout our lives as protectors and guides, especially during periods of stress. Much conjecture as to what they are or where they come from. Some believe that they live among us, others believe they are literally sent from a Godlike presence in the universe. It also seems they are classified as dark angels and angels of the light and have a hierarchy of power. It is conceivable that one in five people have encountered an angel at least once in their lifetime.

Apparition: A ghostly figure that can be sensed, seen, heard, smelled, or felt. Can be in the form of a ball of energy, a wisp of smoke-like substance, or in solid form; in any case, a deceased individual or animal spirit entity with enough material energy and motivation to make contact. This entity can be benevolent or malevolent, confused and frustrated, or simply a spirit force without a clue of purpose; also known as a specter, shade, spirit, or ghost. Possibly one in six individuals have brushed shoulders with an apparition at least once in their lifetime.

Apport: Objects such as flowers, small animals, or things that are physically transported or exchanged to and from the otherside by an advanced medium with exceptional abilities during a séance or demonstration.

Astral body: The etheric, spiritual, or nonmaterial body possessed by all human beings that continues to function after a person's physical death; it is also the body double that experiences an Out of the Body Experience (OBE).

Astral planes: The planes or levels of the spirit world where the next existence commences for the deceased. As many as ten and as few as four successive planes have been conjectured.

Astral projection: Out of the Body Experience (OBE). This is when the astral body temporarily slips away from the physical body and travels where the mind wants it to go; this state can be induced by illness, trauma, emotion, or desire. Occurs often in deep sleep.

Astrology: The ancient art of forecasting future events for people and places by studying the stars and planets and their influences; this is done by complicated mathematical formulas, birth dates, star and planet alignments, and their particular influences; some astrologers "cast" by divination methods. Today, some aspects of astrology are handled by computer, especially formulas. Many astrologers using computers claim that they provide more accurate and thorough information.

Aura: A luminous, colored envelope (or halo) that surrounds all living things that emit vibrational energy. Sensitive individuals can discern these auras in others, in particular the colors that change with moods, health, and activity. Others can feel or sense the vibrations of energy emitting from others without seeing the colors or the aura itself.

Automatic writing: Usually done by a medium in trance; this is rapid writing done on sheets of paper, the communication or pictures being received from the spirit world.

Bardo: When the deceased is in a limbo (a state of nothingness, suspense) status; the place between death and rebirth; a Buddhist term having to do with reincarnation.

Bilocation: This happens when a living person is seen in two different places at the same time and both "bodies" appear as solids. Some thinking on this is that a person who unknowingly sends out his body double to another location is in some sort of deep trance.

Brain waves: The brain gives off measurable electrical impulses or currents of electricity. Beta waves are the norm when you are awake. Alpha waves occur when you are distracted, "star gazing," or daydreaming; Theta waves happen when we enter dream sleep; Delta waves occur when we are in deep sleep. Theta waves transpire in meditation and are very likely to lead to a trancelike state. When Delta waves intertwine with Theta waves, OBEs can occur. Alpha brain waves seem to be the entry point for entering into intuition, prophecy, and insight.

Brujo *(brew ho)***:** North American Spanish for a sorcerer or soothsayer, different from a diablero, which is a wizard sorcerer with evil powers and intent. A brujo is a medium-healer.

Cayce, Edgar: "The Sleeping Prophet." An amazing American psychic and medium known for his verified psychic healings of patients while in trance. He was not a doctor yet was able to assist over 30,000 clients (many located considerable distances away) in need of physical and emotional assistance. He was an advocate of homeopathy and herbal medicines. He was also a user of the Akashic Records and often did his research on clients and patients, reincarnation, and prophecy in the universe's "library" of souls.

Chakras: A term from ancient India; there are seven major chakras (energy centers) in the human body, from the top of the head down to the tail bone, in a straight line, where energy enters and leaves. Roughly, these chakras are the universal life force in all of us; they are different colored vortices that penetrate the aura and appear to be extremely important for movement of energy (prana) and vibrations. Author recommends further research into this area.

Channeling: Frequently mistaken for mediumship; channelers communicate, usually in a state of trance with beings in the universe; whereas the (spirit) medium contacts "dead people." Channeling is a very old craft that has been used in prophecy for thousands of years.

Ch'i (Chi): An ancient Chinese term for the body's energy force. The human body is broken down into many meridians (divisions) where ch'i enters, circulates, and leaves. Acupuncture is the medical art of fixing or redirecting this energy force.

Clairaudience: French for "clear hearing"; specifically, picking up noises and spirit voices.

Clairsentience: The ability of picking up feelings about places, people, and things—"that certain feeling."

Clairvoyance: The ability to see and perceive spirits, events, and insight.

Cold spot: Term used for a cold area where spirits or ghosts are present; temperatures can drop as much as thirty degrees in a few minutes; conversely, a warm draft can also appear announcing a spirit presence.

Control: A medium's spirit guide or a familiar entity that acts as the go-between in contacting or communicating with a spirit(s), or the spirit world.

Cryogenics: The controversial science of freezing dead human bodies or heads for the hopeful purpose of restoring them to life and better health in the future, when medical advances find cures.

Cryptomnesia: Belief that the brain retains everything that is ever heard, not heard directly, felt, smelled, thought, seen, and all actions and physical movements taken—from the womb to the present, consciously or unconsciously; it is thought that visions and intuitions come from the brain's memory capabilities of retention when certain stimuli are activated.

Déjà vu: French phrase for "already seen." It's a feeling that you have been there or done a certain thing before.

Demons: Evil or bad spirits that can interfere in a person's life. It is not known if they ever lived, where they come from, or how they make entry into the earth plane. Demons thrive on our fear and seemingly live from the subconscious encouragement we unwittingly give them.

Dharma: The supreme operating law of the universe and takes power over all beings. Truth, duty, goodness, and virtue; when a person lives, believes, and practices dharma, they stand a good chance of erasing negative karma. Important for reincarnation.

Dimensions: Conjecture arises over how many dimensions exist; currently being theorized by quantum mechanics; traditional science states three: width, breadth, thickness; others make four: width, breadth, thickness, and time; with new physics, the superstring theory, a fifth dimension might be added: gravity. The superstring theory might include as many as ten dimensions or more. What is important to occultists is that the fifth and other proposed dimensions are where the otherworld or astral planes are located and that these dimensions overlap.

Discarnate: A disembodied entity or spirit; an individual that has crossed over and is now in spirit.

Divination: Foretelling of future events by prophecy, spirit communication, and intense intuition.

Doppelganger: German for a "double walker." This is the "troubled" double of a person who is living; lots of speculation on how and why this occurs, and why this "wraith" does not have the best of intentions. This double appears to be a physically complete duplicate.

Dowsing: Use of a special divining rod to find underground minerals and water; some dowsers further use the rod to connect and communicate with forces of the universe.

Dreams: An exceedingly important avenue for prophecy, spirit communication, and messages. Theta and Delta brain waves occurring in sleep often stimulate these phenomena.

Druids: A large Celtic priestly caste (men and women) that covered much of northern Europe in prehistoric and Roman times. They were deeply involved with nature, the environment, and trees; *Druid* means "knowing the oak tree." They exerted considerable influence over the European tribes because of their remarkable gifts of prophecy and their knowledge of science, planting times, the calendar, astronomy, herbal medicines, and mediumship. They could be considered true witches, soothsayers, magicians, and wizards. Druids were supposedly skilled in "shape shifting," which is changing into animal forms at will. They had a gruesome habit of human sacrifice, which caused the Romans to eliminate them (political reasons also). Merlin, the magician of King Arthur, and Wicca survive as reminders of the Druids— they also have adherents today. Ancient Druid customs still lend color and custom to our various holidays and ceremonies.

Earth-bound: Being unable or unwillng to leave our earth plane after death. Earth-bound spirits are held back from the other higher planes because of evil deeds, materialism, confusion, lack of knowledge of how to transmigrate, or a deep attachment to loved ones left behind. Some don't realize or accept their deaths. Many of these spirits end up haunting our plane.

Ectoplasm: A fluidlike substance emanating from the body orifices of a medium that appears in a physical form such as of a face, body, or body parts. Bright light dispels ectoplasm, and it is odorless, gooey to the touch, and chalk-white to smoky in color. Spirits produce this substance in order to show us who they once were, physically. It also appears that some of these materializations are fraudulent. The production of ectoplasm seems to be a lost art among current mediums.

Electronic voice phenomenon: Electronic voice contact and communication by spirits from tape recorders, a voice-activated tape recorder, telephone, radio, or computer; could be considered controversial except for the large number of people who have had the experience of receiving these messages; very difficult to explain away.

Elysian Fields: Ancient Greek version of a delightful and blissful paradise meant for exceptional people, heroes, and warriors, which is almost similar to a Summerland concept.

Energy scars: Residue or vibrational energy that is left behind from past lives or events in the places where they once lived or where events such as battles once occurred.

Eternity: Infinite time; immortality; forever.

Ethereal body: The human body's invisible double, which is attached during life and detached when the living body dies; many consider this double to be the soul of the person. Held to the living body by a silverlike cord at the top of the head. This is the body or soul force, which advances to the astral planes.

Extra Sensory Perception (ESP): A special awareness outside of the ordinary senses; the sixth sense; the ability to see, feel, and sense things and events beyond what is commonplace. Can be used for mind-to-mind communication and mind reading; mental telepathy.

Feng shui: Chinese art of placement of physical buildings, bridges, houses, etc., and furnishings in their interiors. It is also a system of understanding our place in the universe and has many metaphysical implications covering religion, philosophy, science, and the supernatural.

Free will: The power of choice granted by God or the universe to determine personal destiny or path in life; one's individual decision—right or wrong.

Ghost: An apparition, spirit, or energy force. An individual or animal once alive; a disembodied soul that appears to us in a likeness we can understand. Can be seen, heard, smelled, or felt by some. Much information exists on this subject.

Ghost hunter: Person that attempts communication with spirits. A person who explores certain places where ghosts are supposedly in residence; an attempt is made to identify, classify, and perhaps "release" spirits from the earth-bound state.

Globe: Term used in the occult and paranormal for a spirit's concentrated soul energy mass; comes in various colors but mainly is a small, glowing ball of white light. Some call these "spirit lights."

God: The supreme creator and power of the universe; the universe as the ultimate reality; the sum total of wisdom and goodness in a universe filled with chaos.

Grief psychosis: Medical term or classification for those who are in an emotionally "disillusioned" state over the loss, generally to death, of loved ones or friends; this psychosis term is also used for those troubled individuals who report communication or visits from the desceased.

Guides: Angels, guardian angels, spirit guides; our protection and guidance leaders from the otherside; they represent the good force in the universe. Many stay with us through our lives. According to some, there are also dark angels and guides that come from some sort of a void, bringing bad things and evil forces to plague human beings.

Hades: Another word for hell; the place where earth-bound spirit entities dwell, supposed to be this earth plane.

Hallucination: A sensory perception that has little or no reality; a so-called figment of the imagination induced by stress, emotional anxiety, drugs, sleep (or lack of), or profound desire to experience events that are not real.

Haunting: When ghosts or spirits seemingly frequent or visit certain locales where they once were most comfortable or familiar with; site of a sudden death such as an accident or battle; they can also single out individuals for unfinished business or communication.

Horoscope: A foretelling of future events in a person's life; readings or castings are influenced by positions of stars, planets, zodiac signs, birth dates, and time of birth; very intertwined with astrology. A very ancient art that appears in most cultures worldwide.

Hypnogogic: Drowsiness preceding sleep; a ready state for visions and possible commencement of spirit communications.

Hypnopompic: The semiconscious state of sleep just before waking up; another vision and spirit communication channel.

Hypnosis: A sleeplike state induced in therapy and past-life regressions; much experimentation, research, and readings available on this valid subject.

Hypoxia: Lack of oxygen in the tissues of the body and the brain; this state might produce hallucinations and, according to some medical clinicians, create a false NDE.

Immortality: Survival after the death of the physical body.

Intuition: Instinctive knowing; a hunch, feeling, or insight about something without having knowledge or information.

The invisible world: The spirit world, the otherside, astral planes, Summerland, the fourth or fifth dimensions.

Kabbalah (also, Qabalah): Eleventh-century (probably much older) rituals of Jewish mysticism that remain influential to this day; covers customs, ethics, prayer, and metaphysical and philosophical thought, which can be construed as paranormal in content and practice.

Karma: A Buddhist and Hindu term for the complete ethical and physical consequences of one's actions while in life; the paybacks or rewards, positive or negative, for the soul in the next life. Karma is heavily involved in the reincarnation process.

Karma altering: Bad or good karma can possibly alter a soul's destination in the next life, subconsciously or consciously; much debate here, especially if an individual tries to bring goodness into the world after living a bad life; the damage has already been done and the actions, thoughts, and deeds might not be reversible.

Karmic boomerang: Actions that have been done to others—as well as self—come back, sometimes with a vengeance. "As you sow, so shall you reap," type of consequence; one can only hope that positive actions also come back.

Kirlian, Semyon: The Russian inventor of a special photographing technique that uses high-voltage, high-frequency, and low-amperage electrical fields that processes photographs, showing multicolored vibrations and emanations of auras or biofields, the "Kirlian effect." A complicated photographic phenomenon that points to the existence of an etheric body; there are numerous articles and books on this enormously interesting subject.

Kismet: Arabic term for "fate"; preordained circumstance.

Levitation: Raising objects or people by mind control and supernormal means.

Ley lines: Invisible earth energy lines, many intersecting, that cover the entire planet, almost in precise meridian line patterns, allowing paranormal activity to occur. Could be vortex centers of energy with extreme magnetic flux in which an open doorway to the otherside appears, allowing transportation to past and future. The United Kingdom historically seems to be the host of most of these phenomena. Some compare ley lines to an astral door, where the living and spirit forces can enter and leave known dimensions at will. Stonhenge in England is said to be a site of ley lines.

Life review process: During the early stages of life after death, before transmigration occurs, a spirit guide or angel takes the deceased through a complete, second-by-second review of their entire past life; in Buddhism this is called Bardo, where the soul waiting for transmigration is in a suspended state of limbo. During this process the spirit force or energy force of the soul decides options: whether to go to the astral planes or to remain earth-bound, perhaps even to merge their energy force back into the total matter of the universe. However, those personalities with a lot of "bad weight" remain earth-bound and fail their life review "examination"—through their own decision.

Love: Probably the most important component of the human soul and force of the universe. The key to all spirituality and being. Love of self and others is the finest part of personality and the most rapid path to the astral planes and universal eternity. Love can be said to be the greatest single thing for balance in spirituality and spiritual unfoldment.

Materialization: The appearance of apparitions, spirits, and ectoplasm at a séance or in other settings by other paranormal means.

Maya: A Hindu belief from the Vedanta (a holy book of that religion), that everything in our world is an illusion.

Meditation: The act of focusing the mind in contemplation; a peaceful state of listening to the environment, surroundings, and universe; a state of openness to messages and communication with the inner mind and spirit guides. Intense focused meditation can lead to an altered state of consciousness. Meditation is listening. Through intense meditation, prophecy, healing, and spirit contact can be attained; meditation is the portal to psychic ability.

Medium: A gifted person who is receptive to supernormal things; also a person who acts as a go-between with the deceased; a "sensitive" who conducts séances and readings, delivers prophecy, renders healings, and one who might be able to produce physical manifestations.

Metaphysics: A highly abstract branch of philosophy that deals with the supernormal, supernatural, unseen, and unknown features of our lives and the universe, or in other words, ontology, cosmology, the mystical and transcendental; also deals with the abstracts of being and the meaning of everything;

Metta: A Zen Buddhist prayer of loving-kindness said for people that hold few beliefs, perhaps are unkind, confused, or disliked. It is a prayer sent in love.

Mystic: A person attempting to find union with the occult, supernatural, God, the universe, ultimate reality, insight, intuition, purpose, or inner-self; mystics remove themselves from society's mainstream while looking for a higher purpose. Many famous individuals throughout mankind's history have been mystics.

Near Death Experience (NDE): Occurs when a person who is considered dead from trauma or other occurrences, detaches from their body and goes into the "light." Some go through a tunnel and appear on the otherside where they meet angels, Godlike persons, guides, and deceased relatives. Many claim they didn't wish to come back, but all were forced back to life again. A few did not have the best of experiences, saying that they now knew what hell was about. Medical clinicians claim these experiences are from hallucinations, hypoxia, and medication. NDEs have occurred throughout history, in all cultures and religious persuasions, and have been experienced by vast numbers of people.

Necromancy: An archaic word for contact or communication with the dead to find out facts of the present or future for possible misuse or personal gain; this is not a flattering term and can also be construed as worship of the dead or death.

Necrophobia: An intense fear of death, dying, or the dead.

Nostradamus, Michel: Sixteenth-century medical doctor and prophet; he made numerous prophetic predictions disguised in obscure poetic quatrains for fear of being branded a witch and heretic; his method of prophecy was devised by scrying or looking into a cauldron filled with water. A very interesting subject to study.

Nirvana: From Buddhism; the ending of the cycle of positive reincarnation and karma; the final extinction of all human emotions and the end of individual consciousness. This is when the human personality meets oblivion and merges totally with the universe, the desired final paradise and resting place of the extraordinary soul. Mainly achieved through many reincarnations.

Occult: Matters that deal with the supernatural and paranormal.

Ouija Board: (French *oui* for yes, and German *ja* for yes) An occult gamelike board with the letters of the alphabet and a movable device (planchette) used to slowly spell out spirit messages and communication. It's used both for parlor games and by serious students of spirit communication; many in the "field" of the paranormal consider this device for spirit contact to be a dangerous tool in novice hands because of the dangers of communicating with lower forms of spirits.

Out of the Body Experience (OBE): Also known as astral projection; temporary movement of the ethereal body out of the physical body; usually occurs during sleep, stress, or in an altered state of consciousness. Usually remembered by the participant and doesn't seem to be a harmful experience. The person experiencing the OBE appears to be able to travel considerable distances and some note their etheric body is able to communicate with people.

Parallel world: The astral world or otherside running parallel to our current dimensions of reality.

Paranormal: Another "loose" word for the supernatural; occurrences that are beyond rational scientific explanation.

Parapsychology: A rational study and logical method of investigation of clairvoyance, psychokinesis, and mental telepathy; a division of psychology that goes beyond the study and investigation of the human psyche.

Past-life regression: When an individual is in a state usually induced by hypnosis and supervised by a hypnotist or certified clinician and regresses to previous lives; this is an interesting endeavor for those wishing to relive previous lives, seek treatment of current phobias or illnesses, or at least attempt to identify these problems, and for those who are interested in reincarnation. Can be an amazing or a lukewarm experience.

Poltergeist: German for "noisy ghost." A noxious, noisy spirit entity or mischievous ghost who is responsible for breaking things, stirring up households, and causing trouble—sometime serious. It is felt that these troublesome spirits are brought forth by troubled, early pubescent girls and sometimes, boys. There is considerable information on this activity.

Prana: A Hindu/Buddhist term for energy that is in all physical matter in the universe, which also includes human beings; that special "spark" that energizes everything.

Prayer: Communication in word or thought with a higher being in the universe.

Precognition: Premonition, foreknowledge, prophecy; a knowledge of future events before they happen, big or small picture.

Premonition: A sense or precognition that something will happen.

Prophecy: Seeing into the future; sometimes the information comes in several sequences and fragments, can be full-blown with colors, names, faces, events, dialogue, even dates and times. Mediums and some psychics can be very good at receiving this information, which usually comes through in meditational trances or scrying; can be divine revelation.

PSI: The study of psychic phenomena, especially psychic experiences like ESP.

Psychic: A person who is sensitive to nonphysical and supernatural forces; can have the insight to see beyond the physical world, such as into the future, and is very adroit at feeling paranormal occurrences and influences.

Psychic Detectives: Psychics that assist police forces and clients in solving crimes or locating missing persons; some even branch out into locating archaeological sites.

Psychic Healing: Physical and emotional healing by gifted mediums, psychics, and healers by way of spirits or by tapping into the power of the universe; has become a staple in hospitals recently, but has been used by mankind for thousands of years.

Psychic scars: Energy residue left behind from past events and individuals; see Energy scars.

Psychokinesis (PK): The movement of objects by mind control; "mind over matter."

Psychometry: The act of ascertaining facts or "seeing" past or future events by feeling an object.

Quantum mechanics: Very simply defined, general theories dealing with interactions of all matter and energy in observable quantities; is composed of numerous theories in physics, many new, one of which involves transference and transformation of energy. Quantum mechanics is ever changing—and rapidly is garnering theories of the universe, structures, mathematics, energy, molecules, atoms, dimensions, etc. This system, in its reevaluation of physics, has gone far beyond the old tried-and-true scientific rationale and is far more exploratory. Many students of the paranormal are interested in the rapidity of its discoveries, eventually believing this discipline will discover the otherworld. This area of physics is currently undergoing an explosion of knowledge and findings, and if the energy and direction remains constant and unfettered, we will continue to be astounded by new revelations of the universe, perhaps even our place in it.

Reiki *(ray-ke)***:** A natural healing method based on tapping into the energy field of the universal life force, usually by a hands-on method, from certified Reiki practitioners. Reiki healing can also be done by remote means (there is no space or distance), through intense visualization. Healing by this method requires focused concentration while the ch'i energy field is manipulated.

Reincarnation: The belief held by many millions of people and certain religions of the world that human souls are reborn in new physical bodies for another life, sometimes many times, similar to a revolving door. The purpose of reincarnation is to learn from past mistakes or to purge negative karma, eventually going to higher astral planes, concluding these many life experiences, after negative karma has been completely eliminated, with entry into Nirvanna. There are many case studies on reincarnation that do not take in the considerations of continual rebirth. Strongly recommend research on this vast subject because of many varied beliefs.

Remote viewing: When the "third eye" or inner eye (inner self) is able to see beyond the physical body. Remote viewing uses the mind to see a place, an object, event, or a person, and is similar to the mind undergoing an OBE. Remote viewing was experimented on and used by Russian (Soviet) spy organizations as well as by the American CIA. Numerous books have been published on this subject; however, most of the information from these experiments is still classified as secret.

Rescue circle: A group of like-minded individuals gathered for the express purpose of giving relief and release to a ghost/spirit, encouraging the spirit to "move on" to an astral plane. This is usually done by words and a special ritual.

Revenants: These are ghosts/spirits/entities who return from an astral plane for unfinished business and curiosity after a long absence. They can be a malevolent force, but not necessarily, drawing energy from the living's psychic energy. They appear to be indiscriminate about whom they encounter for this drawdown of energy. They are comfortable in locations they once were most familiar with.

Samsara: Hindu and Buddhist term for the great cosmic wheel of life, death, and reincarnation. As humans we are meant to be filled with joy, suffering, pain, evil, goodness, and discovery; we then die, evaluate the sum total of accrued karma, and rejoin this seemingly never ending cycle of "enlightenment." Once total enlightenment is achieved, according to Buddhism, the journey to Nirvanna can commence.

Santeria: A religious and magical practice that originated in Africa; it is a combination of West African religious rites and Roman Catholicism that blended (in the Western Hemisphere), resulting in a form of Voodoo. It is practiced in several Latin American and Caribbean countries, and in other forms in Africa.

Scrying: The process of receiving cosmic information during meditation or trance by way of crystal balls, mirrors, candles, and bowls filled with water (reflective surface)—used by Nostradamus. A very old craft used for hundreds of years (maybe thousands) for spirit communication, prophecy, and a subconscious response for the purpose of solving problems, looking for solutions, and seeking answers. Can also be likened to having the "second sight."

Séance: French for "sitting." The séance is a formal gathering or meeting of two or more like-minded individuals for the express purpose of communicating with the spirits of the dead and/or entities. A chosen séance medium acts as the communicator and receiver during these sessions.

Sensitive: A person who is a medium or psychic, and possibly any individual who has the ability to communicate with spirits and who is also attuned to paranormal phenomenon.

Shakabuku: A Japanese Zen phrase for a "spiritual kick," meaning to get back on the path of spirituality and enlightenment.

The sight: The sixth sense of intuition; strong psychic abilities.

Sixth sense: Going beyond the basic five senses of seeing, feeling, tasting, smelling, and hearing; this is the sense of intuition, sight into the otherworld, awareness of spirits, and the prediction of future events; the state of having "the sight" and "second sight."

Soul: The very essence of the human personality, which survives physical death; the spirit; the energy force; the sum total of morals, emotions, skills, knowledge, and abilities that accrue from an individual's life; contained in the brain's shared mind while alive and separated from the physical brain in death.

Spirit: A soul; a disembodied entity; a discarnate entity; the energy force of a deceased individual and animal. The sum total of the essence (personality) of a human being that survived physical death.

Spirit lights: Light, faint or bright, emitted from the energy of a spirit; can be seen as several small, twinkling, white lights or as a small globe of light. Some observers have claimed other colors such as faint orange, blue, and green.

Spirit photography: Photographs taken of spirits/ghosts on purpose or by accident. Became very popular during the late nineteenth century and fell into disrepute almost immediately due to fraud— double exposure and additions. Many spirit photographs exist from this period and some appear to be authentic. With the sophistication of modern photographic equipment and techniques some exceedingly interesting spirit images now exist.

Spirit team: A group of spirits that assist a living individual; can be made up of a doctor, guide, chemist for health and happiness, a learned advisor, etc. The size and makeup of team depends on the needs of the individual, switching specialized advisors based on needs at the time.

Spiritualism: A pseudo-Christian religion and collection of paranormal beliefs. Belief that spirits from death survival do exist and can be contacted by the séance and medium; that there is another active world and life after this one. Spiritual healing is a gift from the otherside and can help the living. Spiritualism originated in the 1840s in the United States and rapidly spread through many parts of the world. It thrives today in writings, thoughts, and practices, as well as in certain philosophical aspects adopted by other churches. There are formal Spiritualist organizations with numerous congregations throughout the world today, bound with a code of ethics. Brazilian Spiritualism walks hand-in-hand with the Roman Catholic Church. The church and movement of Spiritualism has a considerable list of tenets that center around God, the universe, and many past religious leaders and founders, such as Jesus.

Spirituality: A person's morals, ethics, beliefs, actions, and deeds. The main facets of spirituality are compassion, love, and forgiveness—to yourself and others—also the belief that we die the way we've lived.

Spirit whispers: Spirit(s) attempts to contact through dreams, intuition, or that "certain feeling," for the purpose of warning, comfort, inspiration, and assistance; can also be from lower forms with a "bad" agenda.

Study circle: A group of like-minded people that meet on a regular basis for studying, training, and practicing the séance, also for healing and paranormal discussions.

Summerland: The astral plane of paradise, or heaven, in the invisible world, where a person who lived a good life goes after physical death. It is the place of orientation and indoctrination. Discovered through dreams and spirit visits by the "Poughkeepsie Seer," Andrew Jackson Davis in the 1840s.

Synchronicity: A term introduced by Carl Jung to express the idea that there are no meaningless coincidences; everything is connected by mind and matter; coincidences are interrelated and meaningful; events—personal and big picture—simply don't happen by random accident; everything is tied together for reasons that later become more apparent.

Table tipping: A very popular method of psychic ability and demonstration in the early days of Spiritualism in which several people place their hands (vibrational energy) on a table, and with spirit assistance, the table moves and levitates throughout a room; this movement is to demonstrate the spirit's energy and communication skills. This method of spirit contact is used less frequently today.

Tao: The ancient Chinese process of linking humans and the universe through philosophy and metaphysics by interaction; a way of social and intellectual living.

Tarot cards: A special deck of 78 colorful cards used by tarot readers and psychics for divination, intuition, self-help, readings, prophecy, and demonstration of psychic ability. A very popular and old method of looking into past, present, and future events.

Telekinesis: The mental ability to move physical objects without the use of any known physical force; also called teleportation, and is a form of psychokinesis. This method of mind control and power demonstration was used by the Soviets (Russia) in research and actual demonstration but is another one that is classified as "secret."

Telepathy (Psi): The ability of mind-to-mind contact (ESP)—close and far away, seeing into the future (precognition, prophecy), clairvoyance, and telekinesis; scientists are studying these psychic phenomena in laboratory experiments and have not yet been able to draw any empirical conclusions as to how and what these abilities are and why some individuals are able, or appear able, to demonstrate these abilities.

Theosophy: A philosophy, doctrine, and movement that originated in 1875, combining ancient Egyptian mysticism; Buddhistic and Brahmanic (Hindu) religious doctrines; and theories of reincarnation, divination, and clairvoyance. Very interesting movement with unusual personalities that would be very worthwhile research material for students of the paranormal and occult.

Third eye (Mind's eye): A chakra point (ajna), which is located between the eyebrows and is the center for all psychic abilities; this chakra point is associated and energized with/from the pineal and pituitary glands.

Trance: Deep meditation, apparent sleep, or unconsciousness—when the mind is at rest, mental activity is given free rein. Used by mediums, mystics, and psychics for intense clairvoyance and clairaudience purposes. Through deep trance, the medium allows the spirits to take possession and speak using their vocal cords.

Transfiguration: The change occurring from physical death to spirit energy form or mass.

Transmigration: Movement from one astral plane to another.

Visions: Intuitive insight, particularly with prophecy (future events), prediction, "knowing" in the mind; impressions of future events through the mind's eye; predictions can come from trances and dreams.

Vortex centers: Another term for ley lines or energy centers; controversial; an invisible pattern of energy lines or meridians that cover the earth. Some believe that a passageway to and from the otherside (astral door) can occur and that one can travel to the past and future.

White light: A mental thought or vocal oath of protective God light, which is envisioned to surround a participant(s) during the séance, meditation, sleep, or spirit communication, for protection from unwanted lower form entities; is used by many practitioners of the occult arts on a daily basis for protection against evil or bad happenings.

Wicca: White religious witchcraft; Wicca is the Old English word for witch; Wicca is sorcery, spells, and divination (prophecy and soothsaying), without any malevolency or evil intent. Closely associated with the Druids, it is heavy in environmental issues. Wicca is practiced in Europe and North America and has strong ties with Goddess (ancient pagan religion involved with mother earth) cults and movements.

Yin and yang: From ancient Chinese cosmology. Yin is the feminine aspect of life in the universe; Yang is the masculine. When they are balanced, all is in harmony. Yin is darkness, cold, and wetness; whereas Yang is light, heat, and dryness. Both combine to produce all whatever comes to be in the universe.

Zen: Japanese word for meditation; a sect of Buddhist mysticism that is popular throughout the world. Zen is composed of philosophy and a way of living without theology, although Buddhist ritual is frequently incorporated. Zen meditation and development can lead to intuitive wisdom.

Suggested Readings and Videos

Books

The books listed below are a mere sample of the hundreds that seemingly appear yearly in bookstores and metaphysical book and gift stores. I tried to pick the ones that best fit the direction of this book. All of them have merit and are well written; however, the contents of any book and the interest it sparks depend on the reader's needs, in other words, you will seek out what you want.

It requires a vast body of knowledge to be well based in the paranormal and metaphysical arts, and reading books by those authors and practitioners who have the experience is the best way to make your own personal inroad into a fascinating and exciting area.

Allardice, Pamela. *The Art of Aromatherapy*. Avenel, New Jersey: Crescent Books, 1996.

Allen, James. *As a Man Thinketh*. New York: Barnes & Noble Books, 1992.

Anderson, George and Andrew Barone. *Lessons from the Light*. New York: Berkley Books, 2000.

Andrews, Ted. *How to Develop and Use Psychometry*. St. Paul, Minnesota: Llewellyn Publications, 1994.

Bell, Art. *The Quickening*. New Orleans, Louisiana: Paper Chase Press, 1997.

Cliffs Notes. *Dante's Divine Comedy: Purgatorio*. Lincoln, Nebraska: Cliffs Notes, 1999.

Dreller, Larry. *Beginner's Guide to Mediumship*. York Beach, Maine: Samuel Weiser, Inc., 1997.

Dyer, Wayne. *Manifest Your Destiny*. New York: Harper Collins, 1997.

Edward, John. *One Last Time*. New York: Berkley Books, 1998.

Egidio, Gene. *Whose Hands Are These?* New York: Warner Books, Inc., 1997.

Epstein, Mark. *Going on Being*. New York: Broadway Books, 2001.

Evans, Hilary and Patrick Huyghe. *The Field Guide to Ghosts*. New York: Quill, 2000.

Fenimore, Angie. *Beyond the Darkness*. New York: Bantam Books, 1995.

Fenwick, Peter and Elizabeth. *The Hidden Door*. New York: Berkley Books, Inc., 1998.

Fitzgerald, Edward, Introduction by A. S. Byatt. *Rubaiyat of Omar Khayyam*. New York: Book-of-the-Month Club, Inc., 1996.

Geller, Uri. *Mind Medicine*. New York: Barnes & Noble Books, 2001.

Gia-Fu Feng, and Jane English. *Lao Tsu: Tao Te Ching*. New York: Vintage Books, 1989.

Gonzalez-Wippler, Migene. *What Happens after Death*. St. Paul, Minnesota: Llewellyn Publications, 1997.

Gootman, Marilyn E. *When a Friend Dies*. Minneapolis, Minnesota: Free Spirit Publishing, 1997.

Grant, Russell. *The Illustrated Dream Dictionary*. New York: Sterling Publishing Co., Inc., 1995.

Guiley, Rosemary. *Encyclopedia of Mystical and Paranormal Experience*. San Franciso: Harper of San Francisco, 1991.

———. *Encyclopedia of Ghosts and Spirits*. London: Guinness Publishing, Ltd., 1997.

Ham, Bud. *You Are in the Right Place*. Aurora, Colorado: The White Feather Press, 1995.

Hawking, Stephen. *Black Holes and Baby Universes*. London: Bantam Books, 1993.

Holzer, Hans. *Ghosts, True Encounters with the World Beyond*. New York: Black Dog & Leventhal Publishers, Inc., 1997.

Macy, Mark H. *Miracles in the Storm*. New York: New American Library, 2001.

Mann, A. T. *Millennium Prophecies*. Rockport, Maine: Element, Inc., 1992.

McCoy, Edain. *How to Do Automatic Writing*. St. Paul, Minnesota: Llewellyn Publications, 1994.

Meek, George W. *After We Die, What Then?* Franklin, North Carolina: Metascience Corporation, 1980.

Morse, Melvin. *Parting Visions*. New York: Villard Books, 1994.

Norris, Chuck. *The Secret Power Within*. New York: Broadway Books, 1996.

Northrop, Suzane. *Séance, a Guide for the Living*. Brooklyn, New York: Alliance Publishing, Inc., 1994.

Peck, M. Scott. *In Heaven As on Earth*. New York: Hyperion, 1996.

Ramsland, Katherine. *Ghost*. New York: St. Martin's Press, 2001.

Reps, Paul, and Nyogen Senzaki. *Zen Flesh, Zen Bones*. Boston: Tuttle Publishing, 1998.

Robinson, Lynn, and La Vonne Carlson-Finnerty. *The Complete Idiot's Guide to Being Psychic*. New York: Alpha Books, 1999.

Sagan, Carl. *The Demon-Haunted World*. New York: Random House, 1996.

Schnabel, Jim. *Remote Viewers: The Secret History of America's Psychic Spies*. New York: Dell Publishing, 1997.

Schwartz, Morrie. *Letting Go*. New York: Walker and Co., 1996.

Siegel, Mo, and Nancy Burke. *Herbs for Health and Happiness*. Alexandria, Virginia: Time-Life Books, 1999.

Stashower, Daniel. *Teller of Tales: The Life of Arthur Conan Doyle*. New York: Henry Holt and Company, 1999.

Steiger, Brad. *Our Shared World of the Supernatural*. New York: Signet, 2001.

St. Clair, Marisa. *Beyond the Light*. New York: Barnes & Noble Books, 1997.

Time-Life Books for Barnes & Noble, Inc. *Haunting*. New York: Barnes & Noble Books, 2000.

Van Praagh, James. *Talking to Heaven*. New York: Dutton, 1997.

Ward, Tim. *What the Buddha Never Taught*. Berkeley, California: Celestial Arts, 1993.

Waring, Philippa. *A Dictionary of Omens and Superstitions*. London: Souvenir Press, 1997.

Williamson, Linda. *Contacting the Spirit World*. New York: Berkley
    Books, 1997.
Zukav, Gary. *The Seat of the Soul*. New York: Fireside Books, 1990.

Videos

Some of the movies listed (mixed DVD and VHS) are less than
"spectacular," but all contain certain elements the student of the para-
normal/occult will consider interesting. Feature films, and made-for-
television movies with paranormal themes are a constant staple that
moviegoers in the United States and many countries world wide seem
to crave.

Among the hundreds of movies that have subjects of interest, I
tried to pick a few that run a wide gamut of interest and subjects; I'm
sure you have your own list of favorites too. Many of these videos can
be rented at your neighborhood video store; others will have to be
purchased through catalogs.

Bell, Book and Candle. (Witchcraft and supernatural) 1958; James
    Stewart, Jack Lemmon, and Kim Novak; 103 min.
The Big Chill. (Spirituality and self discovery) 1983; many stars; 103
    min.
The Changling. (Séance, ghosts, and haunting) 1979; George C. Scott;
    115 min.
Dragonfly. (Near Death Experience and spirituality) 2002; Kevin
    Costner; 105 min.
Fluke. (Reincarnation of animals and people) 1995; Matthew Modine
    and Eric Stoltz; 94 min.
From Beyond: The World of Spirits. (Ghosts, Spiritualism, etc.) 1995;
    no stars; two cassettes, total time of 90 min.
Ghost. (Séance, medium, ghosts, and haunting) 1990; Patrick Swayze,
    Whoopi Goldberg, and Demi Moore; 127 min.
Inner Workout. (Chakras, meditation, and breathing) 1989; Shirley
    MacLaine; 70 min.
Made in Heaven. (Reincarnation) 1987; Timothy Hutton and Kelly
    McGillis; 103 min.
Meet Joe Black. (Death and metaphysics) 1996; Anthony Hopkins and
    Brad Pitt; two cassettes, total time of 3 hours.

Michael. (An angel and death) 1997; John Travolta and William Hurt; 106 min.

My Life. (Spirituality and love) 1994; Michael Keaton and Nicole Kidman; 117 min.

The Others. (Ghosts and hauntings) 2001; Nicole Kidman; 104 min.

Reincarnation—Coming Home. (Reincarnation) 1994; no stars; 48 min.

The Reincarnation of Peter Proud. (Reincarnation) 1975; Michael Sarrazin, Jennifer O'Neill; 104 min.

Séance. (History of the séance) 1997; no stars; 50 min.

The Sixth Sense. (Ghosts/spirits and haunting) 1999; Bruce Willis and Haley Joel Osment; 107 min.

Somewhere in Time. (Time travel) 1980; Christopher Reeve and Jane Seymour; 103 min.

Stir of Echoes. (Death and haunting) 1999; Kevin Bacon; 94 min.

Tai Chi Workout. (Exercise and meditation) 1993; David Carradine; 50 min.

2001: A Space Odyssey. (Rebirth, metaphysics, and the universe) 1968; Keir Dullea and Gary Lockwood; 2 hours and 19 min.

What Dreams May Come. (Death and Summerland) 1999; Robin Williams and Cuba Gooding, Jr.; 114 min.